MW00823776

Rev. Geo. N. Barnes, 715 Clark St. Conneaut, Ohio.

BARNES
GENEALOGIES

INCLUDING A COLLECTION OF

ANCESTRAL, GENEALOGICAL

AND

Family Records

AND

BIOGRAPHICAL SKETCHES

OF

BARNES PEOPLE.

COLLECTED AND COMPILED FROM AUTHENTIC SOURCES

BY

REV. GEO. N. BARNES.

THE RIEG & SMITH PRINTING CO.
CONNEAUT, O.
1903.

LIBRARY of CONGRESS

Two Copies Received

MAR 25 1904

Copyright Entry

Mar. 19-1904
CLASS a XXc. No.
8 2 6 9 b
COPY B

Copyrighted in 1904 by

R.EV. G. N. BARNES,

Conneaut, Ohio.

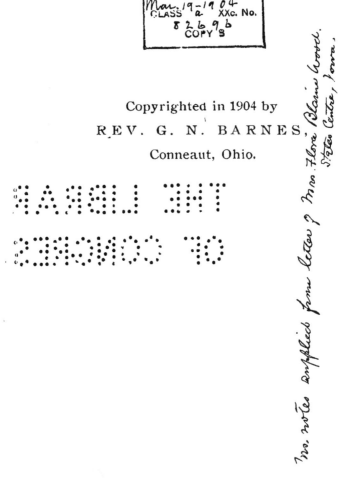

PREFACE.

The desire of many individuals to have a better knowledge of the Barnes people in the United States has induced us to undertake to compile a Barnes Genealogy. Such a work, at the best, will be incomplete and unsatisfactory. The meager and confusing records of Colonial times make it very difficult and tedious to trace the ancestry of families or distinguish the genealogical course from one generation to another. In the rush and hurry of modern times, people have become careless about taking note of passing events, so that frequently, it is difficult to get a family record that will include three generations.

I have given all the ancestral records of Barnes Families of the Colonial period that I could obtain, and genealogical records of several branches of the Barnes Family from 1750 to the present time. The genealogy of Timothy Barnes' Family is nearly complete. All others are fragmentary.

In compiling this work, I have endeavored to make it as authentic and reliable as possible. In seeking for information, I have visited ancestral homes in Massachusetts, Connecticut, New York, Pennsylvania and Ohio ; have had extensive correspondence with the Barnes people ; have spent three days in the New England Historic Library, at Hartford, Conn., and several days in the Congressional Library at Washington.

The most of the statements made and statistics given with regard to the Barnes people prior to 1750 have been gathered from the following : Memorial History of Hartford, Ct., Puritan Settlers of Connecticut, Savage's Genealogical Dictionary of New England, Colonial Records of Connecticut, Historic Addresses, Historic Papers, Church Records of Southington, Ct., History of the Regular Continental Army, Military Record of the War of 1812, American Ancestry, Eccl. and other Sketches of Southington, Ct., by Rev. Herman R. Timlow, Hinman's Ct. Settlers, Virginia Genealogies, by Horace E. Hayden, and History of the Hoyt Family, by David Hoyt. The Colonial records and statistics that are copied direct are printed in fine type, those in full are set off with quotation marks.

G. N. BARNES.

Conneaut, O., Aug. 1, 1903.

CONTENTS.

PART I.
ANCESTRY.

PART II.
GENEALOGIES.

CHAPTER I.

CHAPTER II.

CHAPTER III.

CHAPTER IV.

ELISHA BARNES AND HIS DESCENDANTS.

CHAPTER V.

ISAAC BARNES AND HIS DESCENDANTS.

CHAPTER VI.

JEDEDIAH BARNES.

CHAPTER VII.

THOMAS BARNES OF NEW HAVEN.

CHAPTER VIII.

GENEALOGICAL RECORDS.

CHAPTER IX.

BIOGRAPHICAL SKETCHES.

PART I.

ANCESTRY.

ANCESTORS OF BARNES FAMILIES
OF AMERICA.

The earliest traces of the Barnes race are found in the southeast part of England and indicate a Dano-Norman origin, probably coming to England at the time England was under the Norman kings, 1000–1154. "The name is derived from the Norse 'bjorn' a warrior". (American Ancestry p. 3.) The following is from the family rec. of Charles Barnes, Jr., 1834, Perryville, Ky.: "Records of the church in Surrey, England, show that Barnes families lived there from 500 years prior to the present century. The name is extant there now". (Va. Gen., by Horace E. Hayden, M. A.) Mr. Hayden says that the Barnes families who came from Gt. Britain to New England during

NOTE,— In reply to a question repeatedly asked I will say that the use or omission of e in "Barnes" is a matter of choice or opinion. In all the old records that I have examined there was the same difference in its use that there is now, even with members of the same family.

the 17th century, will no doubt some day be found to have the same origin in the mother country.

The first Barnes people who emigrated to America from England came from Surrey, Middlesex and Norfolk counties.

The following extracts are from early colonial records, and show that at least ten or twelve ancestors of Barnes families came from that part of England to America previous to 1650.

"Edward Barnes was at Elizabeth City, 1623." —*Col. Rec.*

"Launcelot Barnes received 100 a. of Elizabeth City, called the Indian Thicket, 1632. He was burgess for lower part of E. City, 1629-30."--*Md. Arch.*

John Barnes, Plymouth, 1632, prob. of Yarmouth (England), 1639, m. Mary Plummer, had Jonathan, 3 June, 1643. Jonathan, Plymouth, s. of John, m. Jan. 4, 1666, Eliz. Hedge of Yarmouth, had John, Mar. 5, 1669; William, b. Feb. 14, 1670; Jonathan, b. Aug. 27, 1684.—Savage's Gen. Dic.

Joshua Barnes of Yarmouth, England, came to New England in 1632; was one of the founders of the town of South Hampton, Long Island, in 1639; was one of the first settlers of East Hampton (Sag Harbor), 1649; was deputy to the Colonial Court in 1663; had Samuel b. 1649.—Winthrop's Journals, Gen. Dic. and American Ancestry.

Stephen Barnes of Bradford, Ct., b. at South Hampton, L. I., d. at Bradford, moved there about 1700, m. Mary Barnes, had Asa b. Aug. 24, 1745. He was probably the son of Samuel Barnes of East Hampton.—American Ancestry.

Charles Barnes of East Hampton, L. I., 1663, a school-master, was s. of William Barnes of East Winch, near Lynn, Co. of Norfolk, England. He was one of the first settlers of East Hampton.—Savage's Gen. Dic.

Wm. Barnes was one of the original settlers of Salisbury, Mass. The name of Wm. Barnes, aged 22, is found among the passengers for Virginia, Aug. 1635, in the "Globe of London," Jeremy Blackburn, Mr. At the ffrst division of land he received a house-lot and a planting lot of four acres. In Jan. 1640--41 he received the "Rocky Island" in the meadows and other grants. He removed to the w. side of the Powow R. and settled that part of the town called Amesbury. His trade was that of a house carpenter. His daughter married John Hoyt, his two sons, Jonathan and William, died young. He left no son to perpetuate the name.—History of the Hoyt Family.

Richard Barnes, b. and d. at Carshalton, Surrey Co., England, had two sons. Richard and Abraham. Richard, jr., b. 1662, d. 1710, had two sons, George and Charles.

George Barnes came to America in 1695 with his wife, two children and his brother Charles. His second son, Richard, was born at Col. Richard Barnes', near Leonardstown, Md., in 1696.

Richard Barnes m. Penelope Manly; will dated July 15, 1754; died before 1768; children were Thomas, Mary, Rebecca, Sarah, Elizabeth.

Hon. Thomas Griffin, 1733—1785, m. Elizabeth, daughter of Richard Barnes, Tudors Hall, Leonardstown, Md. — *Vir. Geneloagies, by* Horace E. Hayden, M. A.

Abraham Barnes, second son of Richard Barnes, Sr., came to America about 1700 and settled in Maryland; m. Sarah Mc Carty, had one son, Abraham.

Abram Barnes had Richard of St. Mary's Co., Md., d. s., John of Washington Co., Md., d. s., Mrs. Hoe of Hoe's Ferry on the Potomac, d. s. and Mrs. Mason.

Mrs. Mason's grandson, Abram Barnes Thompson, inherited her brother's (Richard Barnes') estate, by taking the name of Abram Barnes.

COL. ABRAM Barnes, of St. Mary's Co., Md., was a member of Albany Congress, 1754, from Md.

TIMOTHY Barnes came from England, died in Conn.: his son was Timothy, d. at Hartford; grandson was Timothy, b. at Hartford, Conn., Apr. 19, 1749. — See *American Ancestry*.

From Church Records at Southington, Conn.
Rev. Jeremiah Curtis, Pastor
Thomas Barnes, Clerk.

Sept. 28, 1743, Ebenezer Barnes, son of Ebenezer Barnes, was married.

Nov. 2, 1732, Gideon Barnes and Mehitabel Shaw were married.

Dec. 3, 1730, Jedediah Barnes and Abigail Warner were married.

Baptismal Records.
Aug. 11, 1740, Josiah, son of Jedediah Barnes.
Aug. 5, 1744, Samuel, son of Jedediah Barnes.

There were ~~three~~ 4 Thomas Barnes that came from England to America previous to 1738 known as Thomas Barnes of Hartford, Thomas Barnes of New Haven and Thomas Barnes of Hingham; who were ancestors of three large branches of Barnes Families in America   Thomas Barnes of Hartford was the ancestor of Timothy Barnes.

THOMAS Barnes, Hingham, 1637, freeman, 1645, came with his w. Ann from Hingham, O. E. (Old England). Had Thomas and John, May 21, 1643; Elizabeth Ann; Hannah; James, b. Apr. 8, 1649; Peter, June 6, 1652.

Thomas Barnes, New Haven, 1643, son of Thomas Barnes, and brother of Daniel of same place: b. about 1623 and d. at Middleton, Ct., 1693. He served in the Pequot war, 1637, was at New Haven, Ct., before 1639, rem. to Middleton, Ct., soon after 1660, m. about 1647. His children were John: Thomas, b. 26 Aug.. 1653: Daniel, 29 Aug., 1659: Abigail: Mabee, born 25 June, 1663.— *American Ancestry*, Savage's *Gen Dic*.

"Thomas Barnes, son of Thomas Barnes of New Haven. had Mary: Thomas,26 July, 1687: Sarah: Rebecca: Abigail: Eliz. 1695: Deborah: Hannah: Samuel, 11 Apr., 1705: Nathaniel, 11 Jan., 1707; Abraham. 1711."—Savage's *Gen. Dic.*

"Thomas Barnes, a soldier in the Pequot battle of 1637, in which 600 savages were killed by 90 colonists, was of Sentinel Hill, Hartford, 1639, sergeant of Farmington train band, 1651, joined church, Jan. 30, 1652, adm. freeman, 1669, was probably the first of the family in America. Name derived from the Norse 'bjorne', a warrior." *American Ancestry*.

"Thomas Barnes, Hartford, 1639, rem. to Farmington, had Benjamin, July 24, 1653, Joseph, 1655, and probably Thomas who m. Mary, d. of Richard Jones."- Savage's *Gen. Dic.*

"Thomas Barnes of Hartford had land distributed, 1640, to him E. of the river and resided there in 1663." — Hinman's *Conn. Settlers*. (See notes on page 16.)

Thomas Barnes(Jr.)m. Mary d. of Richard Jones." *Gen. Dic. of New England*.

"Thomas Barnes was a grandson of John Andrews, Sr., and son of Mary Barnes, d. of John Andrews, of Hartford, Ct."—Hinman's *Ct. Settlers. See notes, P.16.*

Our Old Home in 1861. Sketch from memory by the Author. *See P. 44.*

"How dear to this heart are the scenes of my childhood,
When fond recollection presents them to view!
The orchard, the meadow, the deep tangled wild-wood,
And every loved spot that my infancy knew."

J. J. BARNES and Family in camp at Finley Hot Soda Springs, Cascade Mountains, Ore.

PART II.

GENEALOGIES.

CHAPTER I.

TIMOTHY BARNES, SR.,
HIS ANCESTRY, PARENTAGE AND FAMILY.

THOMAS BARNES of Hartford, great grand-father of Timothy Barnes, Sr., of Southington, was probably one of the first of the family in America. He came to Hartford, Conn., soon after the first settlement in 1635; was in the Pequot war which exterminated the Pequot tribe (the most powerful and hostile of New England savages), for which service he was granted fifty acres of land in 1671. He married Mary, daughter of Thomas Andrews, of Farmington, Conn.; "became a proprietor, by town

NOTE — The Central Congregational Church stands on the east end of the old cemetery where many of the ancestors and first settlers of Hartford are buried. Washington, when on his way to take command of the Colonial army, met the delegation from Boston under the "elm tree." The Athenæum Building is a memorial building, erected on the site of the Nathan Hale homestead, in which are the New England Historic Library, the City Library and many choice relics of Colonial days.

courtesy, Feb. 1639, having six acres allotted to him, where he and his wife, Mary, lived, quite in the north west part of Hartford" (now, the corner of Albany avenue and High street). In 1640—41 they moved to the new settlement of Farmington. He was appointed sergeant of train band, Oct. 6, 1651 ; joined the Farmington church Jan. 30, 1653 ; died, in Farmington, in 1688.

The names of their children were Benjamin, Joseph, Thomas and Ebenezer.[1]

BENJAMIN was born July 24, 1653. His wife's name was Sarah. Their children were Joseph, Thomas and Ebenezer. They moved to Waterbury, Conn., about 1690.[7]

JOSEPH, second son of Thomas Barnes. born 1655, had four children, Jacob, Abigail, Elizabeth and Mary.[8]

EBENEZER, fourth son of Thomas Barnes. was married twice, first wife's name was Deborah, second wife's name was Mehetabel Miller ; had one son, Thomas. He was a deacon in the church ; resided at Waterbury, Conn.

Thomas Barnes, Jr.

THOMAS BARNES, JR., third son of Thomas

Barnes, of Hartford, married Mary, daughter of Richard Jones. They lived in the north part of Southington, Conn.; had a family of five sons and two daughters, Ruth, Samuel, Ebenezer, Thomas, Elizabeth, Joseph and Gershom.[4][5][6]

EBENEZER, second son of Thomas Barnes, Jr., was appointed ensign of train band at the parish of Southington, in Farmington, in 1737; appointed lieut. in South Co., in Farmington, in 1742, and, afterward, was appointed captain the same year; was married; had a son named Ebenezer, who was married Sept. 28, 1743.[11]

GERSHOM, fifth son of Thomas Barnes, Jr., was appointed ensign at New Haven in 1705, and captain of fifth Co. train band in 1753.[10]

Thomas Barnes, son of Thomas Barnes, Jr., and family.

THOMAS BARNES, third son of Thomas Barnes, Jr., was born in Southington, Conn., May 21, 1700; was elected deacon in the church at Southington, Nov. 27, 1728; was also clerk and is supposed to have made the entry on the church record[7] of the baptism of his family when Jeremiah Curtis was pastor of the church in Southington. He died in 1742. His family consisted of eight children whose names were Lemuel, Mary, Nathaniel, Phineas, Irena, Lydia, Timothy and Nathaniel.[12]

Lemuel, oldest son of Thomas Barnes, was born, lived and died in Southington. Conn.

Phineas Barnes was born in Southington, Conn., moved to Great Barrington, Mass., where he lived and died. The names of their children were Phineas, Lemuel, Roswell, Asa, Appleton, William, Thomas. Irena, Vina, Phebe, Lucy and Freelove.

Timothy Barnes.

Timothy Barnes, third son of Thomas Barnes, was born in Southington, Conn., bap. Apr. 1, 1739; married Mariam, daughter of Abraham Miller, March 19, 1760; was appointed administrator of the estate of Abraham Miller in 1765; enlisted in the Continental army, was mustered in Aug. 19, and discharged Sept. 25, 1776. In the spring of '78, in the darkest hours of the American Revolution, he moved his large family into the Berkshire hills of Massachusetts, arriving at West Stockbridge on the 8th of June; he purchased a tract of land in a beautiful valley and on the hillside near, what now is, Williamsville, about one mile west of the village of Housatonic; where he lived until his death.   He died March 12, 1831, aged 92 years.

MARIUM BARNES, wife of Timothy Barnes, was born in Hartford, Conn., May 30, 1737, and died in West Stockbridge, Mass., Jan. 11, 1818, aged nearly 81 years. They had a family of nine children whose names were Silas, Hannah, Timothy, Sarah, Timothy, Elisha, Seth, Isaac, Marium.[13]

NATHANIEL BARNES, youngest son of Thomas Barnes, was born in Southington, Conn., bap. May 1, 1743; was appointed captain of 10 Co., 10 Reg., Oct. 1774; was a freeholder and lived in Southington from 1779 to 1783.[13]

MARY BARNES, daughter of Thomas Barnes, was born in Southington, Conn., bap. May 29, 1737; married a Mr. Mills.

NOTES.

The following quotations are given verbatim in grammar, spelling and language as they appear on the records.

1. "THOMAS BARNES, of Hartford, a proprietor by the town's courtesy: having six acres allotted to him Feb., 1639. He lived on the corner of the highways now Albany Av. and High St. He served in the Pequad war: was granted fifty acres for his service. He removed to Farmington 1639: was sergeant of train band 1651: joined Farmington Church about Jan. 30, 1653. His wife, Mary, was the daughter of ~~Thomas~~ Andros, or Andrews. Their children were Benjamin, bap. July 24, 1653: Joseph, 1655. Thomas Barnes died in 1688." — *Memorial History of Hartford County, Conn.*

"At a session of the General court held in Hartford, Oct. 6, 1651, Thomas Barnes is confirmed Sergeant". *Col. Rec.*

2. Thomas Barnes res'ded quite in the north-west part of the village of Hartford, on land bounded as follows:— On the north and east by the road that leads to the cow pasture,- * He was in the Pequad battle. He removed to Farmington in its early settlement.— *Puritan Settlers of Conn.*

His children were Thomas, Ebenezer and older ones not mentioned. HULDAH BARNES.

3. The following is a copy of the declaration in the "Oath of Fidelity" which Thomas Barnes, with about 360 other citizens, took and subscribed to when Theophilus Eaton was inaugurated governor of Connecticut: "I——doe acknowledge myself to be subject to the government thereoff, and doe sweare be the great and dreadful name of the ever living God, to be true and faithful vnto the same, and doe submit both my person and whole estate therevnto." *Colonial Records.*

While neither the Conn. Constitution or Oath of Fidelity

---

*"The road that leads to the cow pasture" is now, Albany avenue and High street, the finest thoroughfares in the city.

made any mention of the king of England or of the English company which held the royal grant of the lands of Conn.; it indicated a purpose to adhere to the colonial constitution and government, regardless of consequences. This was the first move made for American independence of British rule.

4. Thomas and Mary Barnes lived near Newville Corners in the northern part of Southington, Conn. They had five sons, Samuel, Thomas, Ebenezer, and two names unknown.

—N. E. WARDIN.

5. "Thomas Barnes, son of Thomas Barnes of Hartford, married Mary Jones, daughter of Richard Jones."- *Gen. Dic. of New England.*

6, The children of Thomas Barnes, Jr., were Ruth, b. 1692: Elizabeth b. Apr. 16, 1693: Samuel b. July 8, 1695: Ebenezer, b.Sep. 19, 1697: Thomas, b.May 21, 1700: Joseph b. Aug. 15. 1702: Gershom b. Sep. 13, 1706.—HULDAH BARNES. See *Gen. Dic. of New England*, and *Puritan Settlers of New England.*

7. "Benjamin Barnes, son of Thomas Barnes of Hartford, moved to Waterbury: wife was Sarah: children were Joseph: Thomas, bap. June 8, 1690, at Farmington: Ebenezer, perhaps others." *Gen. Dic. of New England.*

8. Joseph Barnes was a son of Thomas Barnes, of Hartford. His children were Jacob, b. 18 Sep., 1687: Abagail, bap. 23 Feb. 1690: Elizabeth, 9 Oct., 1692: Mary, 17 Feb., 1695. - *Gen. Dic. of New England.*

9. Samuel Barnes, of New Haven, was appointed ensign of train band 1754, and appointed lieutenant in 1758.—*Col. Rec. of Conn.*

10. "Gershom Barnes was appointed ensign in New Haven in 1751, and appointed captain of 5 th Co. train band in 1753 " —*Col. Rec. of Conn..*

11. "In 1718, Ebenezer Barnes, of Farmington, was paid six shillings for killing wolves." - *Historic Addresses.*

"Ebenezer Barnes was appointed ensign of train band at the parish of Southington. in Farmington, in 1737: appointed captain in 1742: appointed lieutenant of South Co. in town of Farmington, in 1768."- *Col. Rec. of Conn.*

"Ebenezer Barnes, son of Ebenezer Barnes, married at Southington, Sep. 28. 1743."- *Church Records.*

12. Thomas Barnes, son of Thomas Barnes, Jr., was elected deacon of the church in Southington Nov. 27, 1728, and died in 1742. He had four sons and two daughters, as follows:– Nathaniel bap. April 27, 1729: Phineas bap. July 12,1730: Irena bap. March 11, 1733: Lydea bap. June 8. 1735: Timothy bap. April 1, 1739: Nathaniel bap. May 1, 1743. *Records of the Church at Southington, Conn.* Jeremiah Curtis. Pastor.

According to the statement of Elisha Barnes. there were two more children. Lemuel and Mary. The oldest son, perhaps. died young: for there is no farther account of him.

13. "Oct. 1765 Timothy Barnes was appointed administrator of the estate of Abraham Miller, of Hartford."--*Rec. of Conn.*

Timothy Barnes enlisted Aug. 19, 1776: discharged Sep. 26. 1776.

Timothy Barnes, Jr., served four days in the Continental army.

Nathaniel Barnes appointed captain of 10 Co., 10 Reg. *History of the Regular Continental Army.*

Silas. b. Dec. 26, 1760: Hannah. b. June 28, 1763: Timothy, b. Sep. 18, 1765 and died Oct. 22, 1765: Sarah, b. Dec. 19, 1766: Timothy, b. Apr. 9, 1769: Elisha, b. March 11, 1771: Seth, b. Feb. 10, 1774: Isaac, b. June 13, 1778: Marium, b. Dec. 4. 1781 and died Jan. 9, 1783. *Record of Timothy Barnes' Family.*

CHAPTER II.

SILAS BARNES AND HIS DESCENDANTS.

SILAS BARNES, SR., oldest son of Timothy Barnes, was born in Southington, Conn., Dec. 26, 1760. He moved with his father to West Stockbridge, Mass., June 8, 1778; was married to Miss Anna Judd; purchased a farm at a place, now called Williamsville, in West Stockbridge, where he lived until his death.

ANNA BARNES, wife of Silas Barnes, born Jan. 28, 1763, was the daughter of Mr. Judd, a Revolutionary soldier.

The names of their children were Elnathan, Silas, Jotham Judd, Alva, Cyrus, Anna, Louis, Charlott and Lucy Mariah.

Cyrus died young.

ELNATHAN BARNES, SR.

ELNATHAN BARNES, son of Silas Barnes, was born in West Stockbridge, Mass., Nov. 13, 1786, died Apr. 7, 1864.

RACHEL BARNES, wife of Elnathan Barnes, daughter of Mr. Brown, was born Nov. 22, 1783. Elnathan and Rachel Barnes were married Dec. 12, 1812, and lived in N. W. Stockbridge, Mass, They had two children, Elnathan and Aaron.

Elnathan Barnes. Jr., and Family.

ELNATHAN BARNES, JR., oldest son of Elnathan Barnes, Sr., was born in N. W. Stockbridge, Mass., Nov. 26, 1823 ; married Elizabeth Bristol ; died May 5, 1887.

ELIZABETH BARNES, wife of Elnathan Barnes, Jr., was born Aug. 9, 1825, and died Feb. 9, 1895.

OLIVE L., daughter of Elnathan and Elizabeth Barnes, and wife of Wheaton Prindel Barnes, was born in West Stockbridge, Oct. 15, 1850, and died at Amboy, Ill., Nov. 10, 1898.

Aaron B. Barnes and Family.

AARON B. BARNES, son of Elnathan Barnes, Sr., was born in West Stockbridge, Mass., Dec. 16, 1825 ; married Lovina Vandusen ; lived in West Stockbridge until 1861 ;

moved to Brooklyn, N. Y. where he died Oct., 1891.

LOVINA BARNES, wife of Aaron B. Barnes, was born in Columbia Co., N. Y., Dec. 15. 1826, and died Oct. 9, 1888.

Their family consisted of eleven children. as follows:— Sidney Bryant, Ransom Augustus, Almond Washington, Arthur Wellington, Hollis Morgan, Dora Pauline, Julia Lovina, Milan Day, Emma Florence, Amos Warren and Matilda J.

SIDNEY B. BARNES was born in West Stockbridge, Jan. 24. 1847; died Aug. 23, 1880.

RANSOM A. BARNES was born in West Stockbridge, Oct. 4, 1848; married Lillie Josephene Merrill Oct. 10, 1886. Their children were Clive Ney born April 9, 1890; died Jan. 23, 1891; and Roy Merrill born Nov. 10, 1891. He is a carpenter, and resides at Tuttletown, Cal.

ALMOND W. BARNES was born in West Stockbridge, Mass., Oct. 12, 1850; married MARGARET RUTHFORD who was born in Perthshire, Scotland, Dec. 6, 1854. Their children are Edna Matilda, born Dec., 12. 1876, and Margaret, born Feb. 16, 1879, at

Brooklyn, N. Y. They all reside at 240 S. Ninth St., Brooklyn, N. Y. He is a prosperous soap manufacturer.

ARTHUR W. BARNES was born in West Stockbridge, Mass., Aug.5, 1852 : died Feb. 4, 1878.

HOLLIS M. BARNES was born in West Stockbridge, Mass., May 12, 1856 ; is married ; has no children : lives in New York ; is a chemist ; places of business, up town store Madison Av., Corner 110 St., down town store West Broadway, corner of Chambers St.

DORA P. BARNES was born Jan. 29, 1858 ; was married in Brooklyn, N. Y., Sep. 1885, to J. C. Dayton. To them were born Mary Thornton, Feb. 19, 1887, and Julia Barnes, Nov. 18, 1889, in Brooklyn. Mrs. Dayton died Nov. 20, 1889.

JULIA L. BARNES was born June 18, 1860 : died Jan. 16, 1890.

MILAN DAY BARNES was born in Brooklyn, N. Y., April 1, 1863 ; is a counselor at law.

ROXANA KEENE BARNES, wife of Milan Day Barnes, was born at Rawdon, Hastings Co.,

Ontario, Canada, Oct. 19, 1859. They were married Aug. 13, 1890. Their children are Clarence S., born at New York City, Mar. 3, 1893 ; and Ethel, born at New York City, July 6, 1896. They reside at 161 Garfield Pl., Brooklyn, N. Y.

EMMA F. BARNES was born at Brooklyn, N. Y., March 16, 1865 ; was married to J. C. Dayton Jan. 14, 1891. There were born to them three sons and one daughter : Charles Henry born at Atlanta, Ga., July 28, 1892 ; William Hale born at Atlanta, Ga., Sep. 22, 1895 ; Harry Almond born at Atlanta, Ga., Sep. 26, 1897 ; Edith Lovina born in Griffin, Ga., Nov. 10, 1900,

JOHN CHARLES DAYTON was born at New Germantown, New Jersey, Oct. 29, 1861 ; was married to Dora P. Barnes Sep. 1885 ; was married to Emma F. Barnes Jan. 14, 1891 ; moved to Atlanta, Ga., and was cashier in the bank at that place until failing health made it necessary to engage in other business. He is farming temporarily at Griffin, Ga.

AMOS W. BARNES was born at Brooklyn, N. Y., March 26, 1867 ; married Miss Sarah

Missimer June 3, 1897; has three children, as follows: Mary Lovina, born May 14, 1898; Amos Warren, born Jan. 23, 1900: a son born Oct. 29, 1901. He is civil engineer and architect; resides at N. W. Corner 9th & Walnut Sts, Philadelphia, Pa.

MATILDA J. BARNES was born Jan. 15, 1870: is a teacher in the Public Schools, and resides at Brooklyn, N. Y.

SILAS BARNES, JR.

SILAS BARNES, JR., son of Silas Barnes, was born in West Stockbridge, Mass., Nov. 19, 1788, and died in Orwell, Ohio, Nov. 14, 1869.

MARY RAWSON BARNES, wife of Silas Barnes, Jr., was born June 14, 1791, and died in Orwell, O. June 22, 1875.

Silas Barnes and Mary Rawson were married in West Stockbridge, Mass., Nov. 9, 1809; moved to Augusta, Oneida Co., N. Y. about 1812; Victor, N.Y., in 1815; Nunda, Livingston Co., N.Y., about 1827; and to Orwell, O., Nov. 6, 1836.

He was an industrious, enterprising farmer. Their family consisted of ten children, as

SILAS BARNES Jr., AND MARY BARNES.

follows: Betsy, Mary, Esther Ann, Maranda, Nathaniel Alverson, Anson Ely, Silas Truman, Harriet Emeline, Eliza Alice and Rachel.

BETSY BARNES, oldest daughter of Silas Barnes, Jr., was born in West Stockbridge. Mass., Feb. 11, 1811; died in Orwell, O.. Aug. 26, 1876.

MARY MURRAY, second daughter of Silas Barnes, was born in Augusta, N. Y., March 17, 1813: was married to John Murray; died in Lenox, O., Nov. 17, 1900.

MARANDA PALMER, fourth daughter of Silas Barnes, was born in Victor, N. Y., Jan. 10, 1818; married John Palmer; died May 14, 1842.

HARRIET EMELINE, fifth daughter of Silas Barnes, was born in Victor, N. Y., Feb. 11, 1822; married, Henry Bedell; died in Orwell, O., Nov. 2, 1852.

RACHEL BARNES, youngest daughter of Silas Barnes, was born in Nunday, Livingston Co., N. Y., May 13, 1833; died in Orwell, O., Sep. 17, 1856.

Esther Ann Runyan and Family.

ESTHER ANN RUNYAN, daughter of Silas Barnes, Jr., was born in Victor, N. Y., Dec. 2, 1814; died at North Shade, Gratiot Co., Mich., March 22, 1898. She was married to Marshall Runyan.

MARSHALL F. RUNYAN was born Sep. 9, 1810; died Sep. 1866. He was a wagon maker. Their children were Mary M., Francis A., Wm. Henry, Harriet M., Geo. A., Adelia Alice, Francis Truman and Emma.

MARY M. CANFIELD, oldest daughter of Esther Ann Runyan, was born June 21, 1835; married W. H. Canfield, March 22, 1855, in North Shade, Mich. Their family is as follows: Ben. F. born Feb. 18, 1856; Lydia L. born Aug. 9, 1857; Fannie E. born Apr. 22, 1858; Geo. W. born Feb. 12, 1861; Elma L. born Dec. 2, 1862. They reside at Lyons, Ionia Co., Mich.

FRANCIS A. RUNYAN, born June 5, 1838; died Feb. 10, 1846.

HARRIET, second daughter of Marshall and Esther Ann Runyan, was born June 5, 1843;

MRS. ESTHER ANN RUNYAN.

married Mr. Proctor ; died Apr. 8, 1866 ; had two children, Katie and Larissa. Katie married Mr. Maddox, and resides at 8515 Vulcan St., St. Louis, Mo.
Larissa died when eleven years old.

WM. HENRY RUNYAN, born Sep. 21, 1840, married Laura Blanchard ; died Feb. 1. 1883 ; left four children, as follows : Frank Runyan resides at 1, Home St., Cleveland. O. ; Fred Runyan, Cleveland, O. : Mrs. Fannie Wolcott, 332 North Union Av., Alliance, O. ; Annie Runyan.

GEO. A. RUNYAN, born Dec. 31, 1845 ; married Emma Jane Cady ; had two sons, Oro, died in 1893, aged 14 years, and Bernie born about 1884 ; is a farmer ; resides at Augusta, Butler Co., Kansas.

TRUMAN F. RUNYAN, born Apr. 29, 1851 ; married in Lyons, Mich., Oct. 5, 1899, to Eutencie C. Robertson ; is a farmer ; resides at North Shade, Mich.

ALICE ADELIA SCHURR, daughter of Marshall and Esther A. Runyan, was born Aug. 9, 1848 ; married Andrew Schurr ; died at Saginaw, Mich. ; had one son named Fred.

EMMA BURNES, youngest daughter of Marshall and Esther Ann Runyan, was born July 18, 1856; was married to Wilfred Burnes Apr. 8, 1889; resides at R. F. D. No. 1. Ionia, Mich.

Nathaniel A. Barnes and Family.

NATHANIEL ALVERSON BARNES, first son of Silas Barnes, Jr., was born in Victor, N. Y., Jan. 8, 1820; came with his father to Orwell, O., Nov. 6, 1836; married Rocina Howard. He was a thorough, industrious farmer; is now living at Lenox, O., strong and vigorous at the age of 82 years.

ROCINA HOWARD was born at Burlington, Vt., July 10, 1821, and died at Orwell, O., Dec. 30, 1897. Their children were Martha, Byron, Lizzie and Hattie.

BYRON BARNES, son of Nathaniel A. Barnes, was born in Orwell, O., May 6, 1846; died in Orwell, O., May 28, 1898.

LIZZIE BARNES, second daughter of Nathaniel A. Barnes, was born in Orwell, O., Jan. 27, 1861; is a dress maker; lives at Orwell, O.

HATTIE BARNES, youngest daughter of Nathaniel A. Barnes, was born in Orwell, O., July 10, 1863 ; is a graduate of the Orwell High School, and a teacher in the public schools ; resides at Orwell, Ohio.

Andrew and Martha Hatch and Family.

MARTHA HATCH, first daughter of Nathaniel A. Barnes, was born in Orwell, O., Dec. 2, 1843 ; married Andrew Hatch.

ANDREW HATCH, son of Daniel Hatch of Lisbon, Conn., was born Nov. 13, 1836.

The names of their children are Lottie L., Clara L., Allen G., Howard A., Roy R., Cornelia M. and Susan R.

LOTTIE L. FOWLER, daughter of Andrew and Martha Hatch, was born Aug. 29, 1862, in Orwell, O. ; married Arthur B. Fowler.

They live at Pasadena, Cal. ; have three children, as follows : Marian R., born July 15, 1892 ; Ruth, born Nov. 25, 1893, and Arthur, born June 8, 1895.

CLARA L. DUNHAM, daughter of Andrew and Martha Hatch, was born at New Lyme, O., May 3, 1864 ; married N. W. Dunham. They live at Joplin, Mo. ; have two children ; Jessie, born Apr. 13, 1892, and Howard, born July 4, 1893.

ALLEN G. HATCH was born in Wayne, O., Feb. 24, 1868 ; married Alta Udell, of Pasadena, Cal., June 24, 1897. They have one daughter, Catheryn, born Aug. 1, 1898. They reside at Pasadena, Cal.

HOWARD A. HATCH was born in Wayne, O., Apr. 5, 1870 ; resides at Norwich, N. Y.

ROY R. HATCH was born in Wayne, O., Oct. 16, 1874 ; married Grace Pitts, of Salem, Mass., Jan. 2, 1897 ; resides at Mt. Hermon, Mass.

CORNELIA M. BEDELL, daughter of Andrew and Martha Hatch, was born in Wayne, O., Apr. 17, 1879 ; married Seth Bedell, June 28, 1900 ; resides at Akron, O.

SUSAN R. HATCH was born in Wayne, O., Nov. 29, 1882 ; lives in Wayne, O.

Anson Ely Barnes and Family.

ANSON ELY BARNES, second son of Silas Barnes, Jr., was born in Victor, N. Y., May 26, 1824 ; moved to Orwell, O., Nov. 6, 1836 ;

married Caroline Loveland; about 1868, moved to Peru, Wis., bought a farm and lived there until 1876. He then moved to Nebraska City, Neb. His wife died Oct. 28. 1893, and he died in Cal., Dec. 12, 1896.

Their children were Hiram, Cyrus, Silas, Ella, Judson and Bertha.

Ella and Judson died young.

HIRAM A. BARNES, oldest son of Anson E, Barnes, was born in Lenox, O., Oct. 5, 1851.

He went to Peru, Wis., with his parents, and, in 1876, traveled from Peru to Charles City, three hundred miles, alone, with horse and carriage; was there joined by his father and brother, Cyrus, and went with them to Nebraska City, Neb., arriving there Nov. 15, 1876. He was married in Nebraska City, June19, 1879, to Ellen Pace, of Elston, Missouri. The following spring, they moved to Syracuse, Neb., where he carried on a large business in a carriage factory. In 1889 he sold out and moved to Cal.; in 1901 he moved to Springfield, Mo., and the next year moved to Sedalia, Mo., where they now reside at 502 North Manateau St. They have one son whose name is Martin Ely.

MARTIN ELY BARNES, son of Hiram A. Barnes, was born at Syracuse, Neb., Apr. 4, 1881; is a blacksmith. His home is at 502 North Manateau St., Sedalia, Mo.

CYRUS BARNES, second son of Anson E. Barnes, was born in Lenox, O., Sep. 25, 1854. He moved to Peru, Wis., in 1867; to Nebraska City, Neb., in 1876. He now resides at 6–11 D St., Marysville, Cal. He is a prosperous, enterprising mechanic doing a large business in a blacksmith and repair shop. He married Miss Alice Martin. There have been born to them five children, as follows: Baby, died young, Ettie, Jessie, Stella and Claud.

SILAS BARNES, third son of A. E. Barnes, was born in Lenox, O., May 11, 1865, died Apr. 11, 1893; married Melissa Hoover.

Bertha Vanderhoof and Family.

BERTHA VANDERHOOF, daughter of A. E. Barnes, was born in New Lyme, Ashtabula Co., O., Sep. 18, 1859; was married in Menomonie, Wis., March 3, 1876, to George L. Vanderhoof, of New Jersey. He was born March 11, 1849. They have lived at Kellogg,

Minn.; Syracuse, Neb.; Nebraska City; Beatrice, Neb.; St. Joseph, Mo., and Portland, Oregon, where they now reside at 576 E. Taylor St. There were born to them five children, Bertha A., Freeman E., Mary A., Ele C. and Daniel E.

BERTHA A. McDONALD, daughter of Geo. and Bertha Vanderhoof, was born at Kellogg, Minn., March 18, 1877; married John McDonald April 10, 1895; has three children, as follows: Hazel Maud, born March 4, 1896, Merl Dewey, born Sep. 22, 1898 and George B. ,born March 30, 1902. They live at Prescott, Washington.

FREEMAN E. VANDERHOOF was born at Syracuse, Neb., Oct. 29, 1878; married Jane Carter Sep. 8, 1901; resides at Portland. Oregon.

MARY A. SLOPER, daughter of Geo. and Bertha Vanderhoof, was born at Syracuse, Neb., Oct. 26, 1880; married Archie F. Sloper, Feb. 16, 1898; had a daughter, Luella May, born June 29, 1899; died in Portland, Oregon, Sep. 8, 1901.

ELE C. VANDERHOOF was born at Syracuse,

Neb., Oct. 18, 1882 ; resides at Portland, Oregon.

DANIEL E. VANDERHOOF was born Sep. 25, 1884 ; died April 26, 1885.

Silas Truman Barnes and Family.

SILAS TRUMAN BARNES, third son of Silas Barnes, Jr., was born in Victor, N. Y., Nov. 17, 1827 ; moved to Orwell, Ashtabula Co., O., Nov. 6, 1836 ; married Julia E. Palmer ; moved to Minn. in 1854 ; died in Winona, Minn., Feb. 13, 1875.

JULIA ESALINA BARNES, wife of Silas T. Barnes, was born in Ausable Forks, N. Y., Nov. 20, 1827.

Five children were born to them, as follows: Mary Esalina, Edward Rawson, Fredrick Palmer, William Percy and Vinnie Zelora.

MARY E. BARNES was born Aug. 3, 1856 ; died June 5, 1866.

EDWARD R. BARNES was born Jan. 13, 1859 ; died Aug. 3, 1860.

FRED. P. BARNES was born in Dover, Minn., Nov. 27, 1861 ; is Master Mechanic on the A. T. & S. F. R. R. ; married Cora I. Geer

March 8, 1894, in Fargo, North Dakota.

Cora I. Geer was born at Lake City, Minn., June 1, 1872. They have two children, as follows:

Helen Geer born January 1, 1895, at Brainard, Minn.

Fredrick Clayton born April 16, 1896, at Brainerd, Minn.

They reside at Albuquerque, New Mexico.

Wm. P. Barnes was born May 1, 1864; died July 4, 1866.

Vinnie Z. Andrews, daughter of Silas T. Barnes, was born in Eyota, Olmsted Co., Minn., Nov. 17, 1868; was married, July 4, 1886, in Winona, Minn., to Ernest John Andrews, of Rockford, Ill.

Ernest J. Andrews, son of John Andrews, is a teacher of Physics in the Robert A. Waller High School in Chicago, Ill. They reside at 5552 Lexington Ave., Chicago, Ill.

Their family consists of two sons and one daughter, as follows:

Frederick Barnes Andrews, born June 15, 1887, in St. Paul, Minn.

Roger Wilson Andrews was born Oct. 21, 1889, in Rockford, Ill.

HELEN LOUISE ANDREWS was born Dec. 30, 1893, in Rockford, Ill.

Eliza Alice Peck and Family.

ELIZA ALICE PECK, sixth daughter of Silas Barnes, Jr., was born in Nunday, Livingston Co. N. Y., Aug. 10, 1830; came to Orwell, Ashtabula Co., O. Nov. 6, 1836; was married to Charles Peck; had two children, Olivia E. and Austin Dean; died in Orwell, O., March 30, 1901. She was a devoted, exemplary, member of the church.

CHARLES PECK was born in Marseilles, N. Y., July 16, 1808; died in Orwell, O. March 29, 1901. His death occurred a few hours previous to the death of his wife, and they were both buried in one grave.

AUSTIN DEAN PECK was born Jan. 20, 1865. He was married to Luella Loomis May 10, 1892. They reside at East Orwell, Ohio.

S. A. and Olivia Townsend and Family.

SAMUEL A. TOWNSEND, son of Isaac Townsend and grandson of Joseph Barnes, of N. J., was born in Spring, Crawford Co., Pa., Apr. 10, 1849. He is a farmer.

OLIVIA E. TOWNSEND. daughter of Eliza A. Peck, was born in Orwell, O., Oct. 16, 1848; was married to Samuel A. Townsend Sep. 4, 1870. Four children were born to them, as follows: Jesse B., Floyd E., Alice E. and Ida R. Their P. O. address is Conneautville, Crawford Co., Pa.

JESSE B. TOWNSEND was born at Conneautville, Crawford Co., Pa., June 29, 1875; married Ethel R. McDowell Feb. 11, 1899; has one son, Everald L., born Nov. 21, 1899; P. O. address is Hickernell, Pa.

FLOYD E. TOWNSEND was born at Conneautville, Pa., Oct. 16, 1878; married Verna Eggleston June 13, 1900; resides at Spring, Pa.

ALICE E. TOWNSEND was born at Spring, Pa., Feb. 15, 1885; lives at Conneautville, Pa.

IDA B. TOWNSEND was born at Spring, Pa. Nov. 29, 1888; lives at Conneautville, Pa.

JOTHAM JUDD BARNES.

JOTHAM JUDD BARNES.

JOTHAM JUDD BARNES, third son of Silas and Anna Judd Barnes, was born in West Stockbridge, Mass., March 21, 1791. About 1810 he was married to Lovina Bradley. They lived in West Stockbridge until about 1815 when they moved to Victor, Ontario Co., New York. In 1832 they moved to Erie Co., Pa., and settled on a farm, three miles south of Girard; cleared up about seventy five acres of the heavily timbered land and got it under a fine state of cultivation; put up farm buildings and a fine two story frame house, set out a great variety of fruit trees, grape vines, small fruit, shrubbery, plants and ornamental trees; making a very pleasant and desirable home where he lived until his death. He died at his old home in Erie Co., Pa., Sep. 13, 1863.

LOVINA BRADLEY BARNES was born Oct. 13, 1787; was married to J. J. Barnes; died at their old home in Girard, Erie Co., Pa., in 1853 at the age of sixty six years.

Her father was a Revolutionary soldier. She said that her husband and herself were

of four nationalities, Scotch, English, Welsh and Irish.

They were devoted christians.

Their family consisted of seven children as follows : Elizabeth Elmina, John Leander, Elias, David Darius, Matilda, Abraham and Sarah.

ELIZABETH E. BARNES, oldest daughter of Jotham J. Barnes, was born in West Stockbridge Nov. 5, 1815 ; died Feb. 26, 1832.

SARAH BARNES, youngest daughter of Jotham J. Barnes, was born June 17, 1831 ; died April 27, 1832.

John L. Barnes and Family.

JOHN L. BARNES, oldest son of Jotham J. Barnes, was born Feb. 25, 1815 ; lived in Victor, Ontario Co., N. Y., until 1832 when he moved with his parents to Girard, Erie Co., Pa. On Jan. 21, 1838, he was married to Julia Ann Goodenow, and, soon after, they moved into the dense forest, in Cussewago, Crawford Co., Pa., into a log house ten feet square. The next year they moved into a good log house where they lived until

Residence of JOHN L. BARNES, Cussewago, Crawford Co., Pa.

1858 when he built a good frame house where he lived until his death. He was a good scholar; taught school several terms; was commissioned captain of the Cussewago Volunteer Militia June 20, 1843, and held the office until discharged in 1849. He was much interested in the public schools, and held the office of school director, after the Pa. School System was adopted, until his death. He was a devoted christian and an active worker in the church. He died at his old home in Cussewago, Crawford Co., Pa., Apr. 15, 1863.

JULIA ANN GOODENOW, oldest daughter of Edmund Goodenow, was born at Sandy Creek, Oswego Co., N. Y., June 27, 1817; went to Elkcreek, Erie Co., Pa., in 1832; was married to John L. Barnes Jan. 11, 1838; went with him to Cussewago, Crawford Co., Pa., and lived with him there until his death. Their family consisted of four sons and one daughter, as follows: Wm. Emory, George Newton, Jotham Judd, Julius Leander and Luanna.

She was married to Willis Hotchkiss Sep. 19, 1875, and lived with him in Spring township, Crawford county, Pa., until his

LUCY A. BARNES. CORA M. BARNES. GEO. N. BARNES. 1886.

death, which occurred June 19, 1881.

She joined the F. W. Baptist church in 1836, lived a Christian life and died in the faith at Conneaut, O., Nov. 25, 1901.

WM. EMORY BARNES was born Nov. 16, 1840 ; died Sep. 30, 1847.

LUANNA BARNES was born Aug. 28, 1853 ; died Apr. 30, 1858.

Geo. N. Barnes and Family.

GEORGE N. BARNES, second son of John L. Barnes, was born in Cussewago, Crawford Co., Pa., Nov. 17, 1843 ; lived on the farm until the fall of the year of 1860 ; attended Albion Academy, at Albion, Pa., in 1860–61 ; enlisted, Aug. 6, 1862, to serve in the War of the Rebellion and was enrolled in Co. (B,) 137 Regiment of Pennsylvania Infantry Volunteers ; was with the Army of the Potomac through the Maryland and Virginia campaigns under Generals McClellan, Burnside and Hooker ; was in the battles of South Mountain, Antietam, Fredericksburg and Chancellorsville ; was discharged June 1, 1863, by reason of expiration of term of enlistment ; returned home and taught school in 1864. He was married to Lucy A. Kidder Nov. 21, 1865; moved to Cranesville, Erie Co., Pa., where he worked several years at his trade in a carriage factory, taught school two terms, was justice of the peace one term and was engaged in mercantile business five years. He attended Hillsdale College in 1869; moved to Wood Co., O., in 1878, and moved to Sherwood, Defiance Co., O., March 19, 1879, where he engaged in the work of the ministry; joined North Ohio Conference, U. B. Church, in 1881; moved to Lake Fork, Ashland Co., O., in 1883; took a transfer to Western Reserve (now East Ohio) Conference and has served the church in this conference as follows: at Lake Fork one year, at Nova two years, at Chippewa Lake three years, at Smithville one year, at Sheffield four years and at Conneaut eight years.

LUCY ANN KIDDER BARNES, daughter of Perry Kidder, was born in Elk Creek, Erie Co., Pa., Jan. 27, 1845; attended Albion Academy two years; taught school in 1864–5 in Elk Creek, Pa.; was married to Geo. N. Barnes Nov. 21, 1865. They have one daughter, Cora May. They reside at 715

Residence of Geo. N. Barnes, 715 Clark St., Conneaut, O.

Clark St., Conneaut, Ashtabula Co., O.

CORA M. WHITE, daughter of George N. Barnes, was born at Cranesville, Erie Co., Pa., Apr. 1, 1872 ; was married to Lewis W. Stentz, son of Daniel C. Stentz, of Ashland Co., O., Oct. 7, 1888 ; had one daughter, Florence Julia. On July 2, 1891, she was married at Giddings, Ashtabula Co., O., to H. A. White. She was a thorough student of music under Dr. Carl Merz, of Wooster, O., and is a good musician and teacher.

HENRY ANSON WHITE, son of Stephen White, was born at Gould, Ashtabula Co., O., July 2, 1869 ; married Cora M. Barnes July 2, 1891. They have two children, Paul Perry and Olive Faith.

Their home is at Gould, Ohio.

FLORENCE JULIA, daughter of Cora M. White, was born at Medina, O., Dec. 2, 1889.

PAUL PERRY WHITE was born at Gould, O., June 26, 1892.

OLIVE FAITH WHITE was born at Gould, O., Sep. 12, 1899.

Jotham J. Barnes and Family.

JOTHAM JUDD BARNES, third son of John L. Barnes, was born in Cussewago, Crawford Co., Pa., Aug. 15, 1846. He enlisted in Co. (B,) 56 Regiment P. V. M., June 28, 1863, and was discharged Aug. 30, 1863.

In 1864–5 he worked for John D. Rockefeller in the I. X. L. Refinery at Oil Creek, Pa. He was enrolled in Co. (G,) 102 P. V. V., March 31, 1865, to serve one year ; saw Lee and Johnston surrender, and was discharged June 28, 1865. He was married to Olive A. Cook May 29, 1866 ; moved to Tontogany, Wood Co., O., March 31, 1868 ; moved from Ohio to Scio, Linn Co., Oregon, started Aug. 22, and arrived at Albany, Oregon, Aug. 29, 1892. He has been engaged in blacksmithing, repairing and manufacturing thirty six years and is at present, in company with his son Jimmie, running a large Carriage, Blacksmith, Repair and Machine Shop at Scio, Oregon.

OLIVE A. BARNES, daughter of Oliver Cook, was born in Elk Creek, Erie Co., Pa., Apr. 18, 1842 ; was married to J. J. Barnes. They have two children, Jimmie R. and Nellie E.

JOTHAM JUDD BARNES.

OLIVE A. BARNES.

JIMMIE R. BARNES.

NELLIE E. BARNES.

Residence of J. J. Barnes, Scio, Oregon.

JIMMIE RILEY BARNES, son of J. J. Barnes, was born at Tontogany, Wood Co., O., Oct. 18, 1873 ; went to Oregon in August, 1892 ; is a machinist, and is Jr. member of the firm of J. J. Barnes & Son, Scio, Oregon.

NELLIE ELIZABETH BARNES, daughter of J. J. Barnes, was born at Tontogany, Wood Co., O., Jan. 15, 1877 ; resides at Scio, Oregon.

Julius L. Barnes and Family.

JULIUS L. BARNES, fourth son of J. L. Barnas, was born in Cussewago Tp., Crawford Co., Pa., Oct. 2, 1848 ; was married to Ophelia Hill June 19, 1870 ; moved to Cranesville, Pa., in 1872, to engage in the blacksmith and carriage business. He was married to Nancy Thrasher Oct. 29, 1874. They reside at Cranesville, Erie Co., Pa.

OPHELIA HILL BARNES, daughter of Martin Hill, was born in Spring, Crawford Co., Pa., in June, 1863 ; was married to J. L. Barnes ; died March 30, 1873. They had one daughter whose name is Erdine.

NANCY THRASHER BARNES, daughter of David Thrasher, was born in Elk Creek, Erie

Co., Pa., March 12, 1855; was married to J. L. Barnes Oct. 29, 1874. They have two daughters whose names are Jessie and Grace.

ARTHUR DELOS MILLS, son of Geo. Mills, was born in Conneaut Tp., Erie Co., Pa., Sep. 29, 1867; was married to Erdine Barnes May 21, 1864.

ERDINE BARNES MILLS, daughter of Julius L. Barnes, was born in Cussewago, Crawford Co., Pa., Apr. 14, 1871; was married to Arthur Mills. They have two children, as follows:

MARGARET OPHELIA MILLS was born in Conneaut Tp., Erie Co., Pa., Sep. 25, 1895.

MILDRED JEANETTE MILLS was born in Conneaut Tp., Erie Co., Pa., March 25, 1899.

JESSIE A. LYON, daughter of Julius L. Barnes, was born at Cranesville, Pa., Oct. 9, 1876; was married to Fred M. Lyon Jan. 29, 1902. She is a graduate of the Albion High School, and has been a teacher several years in the public schools.

GRACE M. BARNES, daughter of Julius L.

Residence of J. L. BARNES, CRANESVILLE, PA.

Barnes, was born at Cranesville, Pa., Nov. 5, 1879; is a graduate of the Albion High School, and is a teacher in the public schools. She resides at Cranesville, Pa.

Elias Barnes and Family.

ELIAS BARNES, second son of Jotham J. Barnes, was born at Victor, N, Y., March 19, 1820; came to Erie Co., Pa., in 1832; married Parmelia Peet Oct. 28, 1841; moved into the forests of Crawford Co., Pa., cleared off a piece of ground and built the first frame house in that neighborhood.

In 1843 he moved to Girard, Pa., where he bought a farm and lived until 1856. He then moved back to his home in Crawford Co.; cleared up and improved the farm, built a new house and lived there until his death which occurred Oct. 9, 1891.

PARMELIA PEET BARNES was born in Portage Co., N. Y., June 23, 1824. Her father moved with his family, with an ox team, from N. Y., into the unbroken forest of Cussewago Tp., Crawford Co., Pa., finding his way to his destination by blazed trees.

Parmelia taught the district school several

ELIAS BARNES.

PARMELIA BARNES.

terms ; was married to Elias Barnes in 1841 and lived with him until his death which occurred five days previous to her own. She died Oct. 14, 1891.

Their children were Martha P., Anner E., Arthur E., Margaret E., Byron B., Elmina A., Charley A., Ella V. and David P.

Martha P. Carnahan and Family.

MARTHA P. BARNES, oldest daughter of Elias Barnes, was born near Crossingville, Crawford Co., Pa., Oct. 12, 1842. In 1843 her father and his family moved to Girard, Erie Co., Pa., at which place she spent the first fourteen years of her life. She improved the good opportunity that she enjoyed and received a good education ; taught two terms of school at Potters Corners in 1859 and, on Nov. 3, was married to Albert K. Greenlee. He owned a good home and farm joining her father's farm to which they moved and lived there about eight years, when they moved to Beaver, Pa., where they were living at the time of his death.

She was married to Thomas Carnahan, of New Vernon, Mercer Co., Pa., Feb. 12, 1880. They moved to York, Neb. in 1884 ;

MARTHA P. CARNAHAN.

pre-empted a homestead near Holyoke, Col.; returned to York, Neb., where they now reside. She is a member of the M. E. Church, a thriving society of six hundred members, in that beautiful little city of church-going people, with its ten churches and fine institutions of learning, without a saloon.

ALBERT KEITH GREENLEE, son of John Greenlee, was born in Spring Tp., Crawford Co., Pa., July 4, 1838, and died Sep. 20, 1870. He was married to Martha Barnes Nov. 3, 1859. Their children were Andrew Keith, Ernest Lot and Ralph Lucas.

THOMAS CARNAHAN was born at Sandy Lake, Mercer Co., Pa., Apr. 27, 1827; married Martha P. Greenlee. They have one daughter whose name is Millie. Mr. Carnahan is one of the proprietors of the roller mills at York, Nebraska.

ANDREW KEITH GREENLEE, son of Albert K. and Martha Greenlee, was born near Crossingville, Crawford Co., Pa., Oct. 25, 1860. His early life was spent on the farm. He attended the State Normal School at Edinboro, Pa., three terms; took a business course in college at Valparaiso, Ind.; went to Sidney, Neb., where he now resides. He is a successful business man engaged in mercantile business at that place.

ELIZABETH MCALLISTER, daughter of Enos McAllister, was born at Glenravel, Antrim Co., Ireland, Dec. 22, 1861; was married to Andrew K. Greenlee May 22, 1888, at Sidney, Nebraska. They have had five children, as follows:

MILDRED GREENLEE born July 15, 1889, died July 18, 1889.

MARTHA R. GREENLEE born Aug. 10, 1890.

KATHERINE GREENLEE born May 22, 1892.

ALBERT D. GREENLEE born Nov. 13, 1894.

ROY E. GREENLEE born Oct. 10, 1897.

ERNEST LOT GREENLEE, son of A. K. and Martha Greenlee, was born in Cussewago, Crawford Co., Pa., July 19, 1863; married Sarah S. Wice; is a blacksmith, by trade, and resides at Prairie Depot, Ohio.

SARAH S. GREENLEE, daughter of B. and J. Wice, was born in Wood Co., O., Sep. 21, 1870. She was married to Ernest L. Green-

A. K. GREENLEE AND FAMILY.
Elizabeth, Catherine, Albert, Martha. Roy and A. K. Greenlee.

lee. Their family consists of four children, as follows :

ETHEL I. GREENLEE was born in Wood Co., O., Feb. 13, 1892.

RUTH M. GREENLEE was born in Wood Co., O., Oct. 2, 1893.

THERON A. GREENLEE was born in Wood Co., O., Oct. 24, 1898.

R. KEITH GREENLEE was born in Wood Co. O., Jan. 23, 1900.

MILLIE WILLIAMS, daughter of Martha Carnahan, was born at New Vernon, Mercer Co., Pa., Aug. 20, 1881 ; graduated in the High School at York, Neb. ; was married to W. H. Williams Dec. 24, 1897. They have had two children, as follows :

BABY WILLIAMS born Nov. 18, 1898, died Jan. 17, 1899.

HELEN MARIE WILLIAMS was born at York, Neb., Apr. 25, 1900. They reside at 119 W. 60 St. Chicago, Ill.

MILLIE WILLIAMS.

ZEALOUS and ANNER SPERRY.

Zealous and Anner Sperry and Family.

ZEALOUS SPERRY, son of Lewis Sperry, was born in Spring Tp., Crawford Co., Pa. He attended College at Meadville, Pa. ; was a union soldier in the War of the Rebellion ; married Anner Barnes ; lives at St. Louis, Michigan.

ANNER L. SPERRY, second daughter of Elias Barnes, was born in Girard, Erie Co., Pa., Aug. 17, 1844 ; moved with her parents to Cussewago, Crawford Co., Pa., in 1856 ; was married to Zealous Sperry May 28, 1864, at Edinboro, Pa. They have two children, Eric Otho and Margaret Elmina.

ERIC OTHO SPERRY, son of Zealous and Anner Sperry, was born in Elk Creek, Erie Co., Pa., June 10, 1866 ; went with his parents to St. Louis, Mich. ; married Addie V. Baughn ; has one son, Lewis Arthur ; was married to Mrs. Emma M. Tucky Apr. 6, 1901. They live at Alma, Mich.

LEWIS ARTHUR SPERRY, son of E. O. Sperry, was born at St. Louis, Mich., Jan. 11, 1891.

MARGARET ELMINA GREEN, daughter of

Anner Sperry, was born at St. Louis, Mich., Aug. 28, 1873. She graduated in the St. Louis High School ; was married at St. Lewis, Mich., Apr. 17, 1895, to Charles A. Green, a member of the Ashley Planing Mill and Lumber Co., of Ashley, Mich. They have one daughter, Esther.

ESTHER GREEN was born at St. Louis, Gratiot Co.,Mich., Oct. 5, 1898.

ARTHUR E. BARNES, son of Elias Barnes, born in Girard, Pa., Dec. 1, 1845, died Nov. 29, 1854.

Margaret E. Leiphart.

MARGARET E. LEIPHART, daughter of Elias Barnes, was born in Girard, Pa., Apr. 11, 1847, and died Apr. 15, 1869. She was married to John Leiphart ; had one son, George.

GEORGE A. LEIPHART, son of Margaret E. Leiphart, was born Oct. 19, 1869 ; was married Oct. 10, 1894, to Gertrude M. Conrad. They have two children, as follows :

CONRAD R. LEIPHART born Oct. 5, 1896,

MARGUERITE E. LEIPHART born May 22, 1898.

Their P.O. address is Munising, Mich.

Byron B. Barnes and Family.

BYRON B. BARNES, son of Elias Barnes, was born in Girard, Erie Co., Pa., March 2, 1848; was married to Ellen R. Cook, at Edinboro, Pa., Oct. 28, 1868; moved to Douglas Co., Kansas, in 1869; moved onto a homestead in Lyon Co., Kansas, in 1870; moved to Wood Co., Ohio, March 20, 1875; moved to Oregon in 1890 arriving at Monmouth on the twenty second day of April.

He was married to Celia Ann Ladow at Corvallas, Oregon, Nov. 19, 1891; bought a fine stock farm of 175 acres, six miles N. W. of Albany, Oregon, where they now reside. The last thirty years he has been engaged in farming and raising stock.

ELLEN R. BARNES, daughter of Olliver Cook, was born in Elk Creek, Erie Co., Pa., Dec. 22, 1850, and died at Bowling Green, O., May 30, 1889. She was married to Byron B. Barnes Oct. 28, 1868. Their children were Mertie J., Forest R., Elma E., Elmer and Jason A. Elma and Elmer were twins. Elma was born Apr. 19, died Sep. 4, 1875.

MERTIE J. STACY.   EARL STACY.   FRANK A. STACY.

CELIA ANN LADO BARNES was born in Pa., Feb. 14, 1852; married B. B. Barnes; had one daughter whose name was Lillie.

FRANK A. STACY, son of W. O. Stacy, was born at Bowling Green, O., Feb. 12, 1868.

MERTIE J. STACY, daughter of Byron B. Barnes, was born at Baldwin City, Douglas Co., Kansas, Jan. 9, 1870; was married to Frank A. Stacy, at Bowling Green, O., Sep. 18, 1889. They moved to Oregon Aug. 28, 1892; have one son, Earl. Their P. O. address is Crabtree, Oregon.

EARL STACY was born at Monmouth, Polk Co., Oregon, Oct. 29, 1894.

FOREST R. BARNES, son of B. B. Barnes, was born in Lyon Co., Kansas, Feb. 14, 1872; was married to Eva S. Towns; is a blacksmith by trade; lives at Monmouth, Polk Co., Oregon.

EVA S. BARNES, daughter of Allen Towns, was born in Redwillow Co., Neb., Jan. 3, 1875; married Forest Barnes. They have one daughter,

KATIE V. BARNES, born in Benton Co., Oregon, Dec. 2, 1900.

EVA S. BARNES.   KATIE V. BARNES.   FOREST R. BARNES.

JASON A. BARNES.

ELMER B. BARNES, son of Byron B. Barnes, was born at Bowling Green, Wood Co., O., Apr. 19, 1875 ; went to Oregon with his father ; married Minnie Hirons at Albany, Oregon, Dec. 23, 1897.

MINNIE BARNES, wife of Elmer B. Barnes, was born in Polk Co., Oreg., July 20, 1880. They have four childen, as follows :

ALTA and ELMA BARNES were twins born at Shelburn, Linn Co., Oreg., Dec. 1, 1898.

OLIVE R. BARNES was born at Wells, Benton Co., Oreg., May 25, 1900.

GLADYS P. BARNES was born at Suver, Polk Co., Oreg., Dec. 20, 1901.
Their P. O. address is Suver, Oregon.

JASON A. BARNES, son of Byron B. Barnes, was born at Bowling Green, Ohio, Nov. 22, 1877 ; went with his father to Oregon ; lives at Walla Walla, Washington.

LILLIE BARNES, daughter of Byron B. and Celia Ann Barnes, was born Sep. 3, 1893, and died Jan. 15, 1899.

ELMINA ANTOINETTE DEICHTMAN, fourth daughter of Elias Barnes, was born in Girard Tp., Erie Co., Pa., Aug. 18, 1851 ; went with her parents to Crawford Co., Pa., in 1856 ; married Charles N. Daniels Aug. 18, 1870 ; married Charles A. Deichtman March 4, 1896 ; is a dress maker by trade, and lives at Saegerstown, Pa.

CHARLES NELSON DANIELS was born Jan. 10, 1850 ; married Elmina A. Barnes Aug. 18, 1870 ; died July 25, 1885.

CHARLES ALBERT DEICHTMAN was born at Saegerstown, Crawford Co., Pa., May 1, 1859 ; married Elmina A. Daniels March 4, 1896. They are members of the Reform Church. Their P. O. address is Saegerstown, Pa.

CHARLES A. BARNES, third son of Elias Barnes, was born in Girard, Pa., Apr. 13, 1853. With him, the love of adventure has been a ruling passion. When a young man he commenced spending the hunting season in the woods in Michigan and the last ten years he has spent nearly all of his time there with his dogs and gun for his companions. In 1898 he bought a lot and built a good house at Crayton, Alger Co.,

C. A. DEICHTMAN.

ELMINA A. DEICHTMAN.

CHARLES A. BARNES.

Mich. His house is well furnished with so-
fa spreads, rugs, robes and coat, made by
himself of wolf, bear and lynx hides ; and
on the walls are hunter's treasures and cu-
riosities of almost every description.   His
P. O. address is Wetmore, Alger Co. Mich.

———

C. FRED HEARD, son of James H. Heard,
was born at Crossingville, Crawford Co.,
Pa. July 23, 1857 ; married Ella V. Barnes.

ELLA V. HEARD, fifth daughter of Elias
Barnes, was born near Crossingville, Pa.,
July 4, 1858 ; married C. Fred Heard. They
live at Scio, Ohio ; have had three children,
as follows :

J. WALLACE HEARD was born at Crossingville, Pa. Sep. 24, 1876 ; lives at Pittsburg,
Pa.

GRACE HEARD was born at Crossingville,
Pa., Dec. 29, 1878 ; is a teacher in the public schools at Scio, Ohio.

JAMES M. HEARD was born Nov. 28, 1879
and died Sep. 10, 1880.

———

DAVID P. BARNES, fourth son of Elias
Barnes, was born in Cussewago Tp., Craw-

ford Co., Pa., March 26, 1860. He was brought up a farmer boy; attended the public school, winters, until 1878, and Crossingville High School two terms; was married to Elnora Sherrod Jan. 1, 1883, by Rev. F. Fair, at Edinboro, Pa.; worked for J. E. Cook from Apr. 3, 1884, to Sep. 30, 1855, and for R. C. Hickernell from Jan., 1890, to Sep., 1893. in a sawmill, the last year as head sawyer. In Sep., 1893, they bought the old homestead near Crossingville, Crawford Co., Pa., where thy now reside.

ELNORA SHERROD BARNES, wife of David P. Barnes, was born in Washington Tp., Erie Co., Pa., Oct. 27, 1863. Their family consists of eight children, as follows:

CARL OLIVER BARNES, born in Spring, Pa., March 30, 1884.

ORA MAY BARNES, born in Cussewago Tp., Pa., March 10, 1886.

GLENN ANDREW BARNES, born in Spring, Pa., March 24, 1889.

PARMELIA ABIGAIL BARNES, born in Spring, Pa., March 13, 1891.

Residence of David P. Barnes, near Crossingville, Pa.

GUY LESLIE BARNES, born in Spring, Pa., March 29, 1893.

FLOYD BURTON BARNES, born in Cussewago, Pa., May 10, 1895.

ANNA ELMINA BARNES, born in Cussewago, Pa., May 19, 1899.

ERNEST BARNES, born in Cussewago, Pa., March 7, 1902.

D. D. Barnes and Family.

DAVID DARIUS BARNES, son of Jotham J. Barnes, was born in Victor, N. Y., March 18, 1820; came to Erie Co., Pa., with his parents in 1832; married Fanny W. Slater; moved to Platea, Erie Co., Pa., where he lived until his death which occurred Jan. 1, 1887. He served his township many years as constable; was a carpenter and joiner by trade.

FANNY W. BARNES, daughter of Benjamin Slater, was born in Madison Co., N. Y., July 14, 1818; was married to D. D. Barnes. There was born to them one son whose name is Homer. Her P. O. address is Platea, Pa.

HOMER S. BARNES.

HOMER S. BARNES, son of D. D. Barnes, was born at Platea, Erie Co., Pa., Oct. 6, 1856. After passing the regular grades in the public schools at home he attended Grand River Institute four years. He has taught school fifteen terms, and served the township in the official capacity of justice of the peace eighteen years. He married Miss Carrie F. Coffman.

CARRIE FRANCES COFFMAN, daughter of J. C. Coffman, was born at Platea, Pa., Sep. 24, 1870. She was married to Homer S. Barnes Apr. 4, 1888. Their home is at Platea, Pa.

Matilda Barnes Smith and Family.

MATILDA BARNES SMITH, daughter of J. J. Barnes, was born at Victor, Ontario Co., N. Y., June 4, 1828 ; was a school-teacher ; married Samuel A. Smith Nov. 1, 1852. Their children were H. Judd and Hiram Arthur.

H. Judd Smith and Family.

H. JUDD SMITH, son of S. A. and Matilda Smith, was born in Girard, Erie Co., Pa., Nov. 12, 1854 ; was bound to and adopted by Mr. Shandrews of N. Y. ; was married to Minnie Chapman ; P. O. address is Coraopolis, Pa.

MINNIE CHAPMAN, daughter of E. Chapman, was born Aug. 31, 1858 ; married to H. J. Smith Jan. 1, 1874. They had eight children, as follows :

I. O., born Feb. 4, 1876, died June 6, 1876.

MINNIE, born Sep. 21, 1877.

ROBERT, born Nov. 1, 1882, died March 20, 1885.

HARRA, born Feb. 20, 1885, died Aug. 18, 1892.

SAMUEL, born July 3, 1887.

NINA, born Sep. 15, 1889.

FANNIE, born Dec. 13, 1890.

MAY, born March 8, 1895.

MINNIE DORMAN, daughter of H. Judd Smith, was married to John Hefferan in 1894. They had one daughter,. Ruth.

She was married to Edwin T. Dorman Sep. 27, 1900. They live at Conneaut, O.

RUTH HEFFERAN was born March 2, 1895.

H. A. Smith and Family.

HIRAM ARTHUR SMITH, second son of Matilda Barnes Smith, was born in Girard, Erie Co., Pa., Feb. 5, 1857; married Martha C. Clark; is a farmer; lives at Fairplain, Erie Co., Pa. There were born to them nine children, as follows:

EMMA MORGIA, born June 8, 1878.

ROLLA C., born May 9, 1879, died July 1880.

Infant son, born Nov. 19, died Dec.. 1882.

MERRIL ELTON, born in Girard, Pa., March 6, 1885.

BURL ALBERT, born Apr. 5, 1887, died Aug. 10, 1887.

MARION ESTRELLA, born in Girard, Pa., Sep. 12, 1888.

FELTON ARTHUR, born May 23, 1892, died Aug. 29, 1892.

ELMA EFFADILLA, born in Girard, Pa., March 9, 1895.

ELDA MANITA, born in Girard, Pa., Feb. 22, 1896.

EMMA M. SPERRY, daughter of Hiram A. Smith, was born in Girard Tp., Erie Co., Pa., June 8, 1878; was married to F. B. Tuckey Apr. 1, 1895; had one son, Arthur Richard. She was married to E. O. Sperry Apr. 6, 1901. They live at Alma, Mich.

ARTHUR RICHARD TUCKEY, son of F. B. and Emma Tuckey, was born in Girard, Pa., Apr. 2, 1896.

ABRAHAM BARNES.

Abraham Barnes and Family.

ABRAHAM BARNES, fourth son of Jotham J. and Lovina B. Barnes, was born in Victor, Ontario Co., N. Y., June 17, 1831. In 1832 he moved with his parents to Girard, Erie Co., Pa., where he lived until 1852 engaged in farming and attending the country schools and a select school at Lockport, Pa. When twenty one years old he with another young man, Giles James, started for the south to teach school. Having traveled for sometime in Tennesee and Mississippi, it being just before the civil war, the growing differences made it desirable that they return to the north which they did by the way of the Mississippi and Ohio Rivers to Cincinnati and from there to Clark Co., O., where he engaged in the lumber business two years and taught school eight years. He was married to Amanda E. Woliston Oct. 2, 1856 near Springfield, O. In 1863 he moved with his family to Lawrence Co., Ill.; purchased eighty acres of open prairie land and by working summers and teaching school winters succeeded in fencing and improving it by erecting substantial house, barn, granary and other buildings. Additional purchases make a total of two hundred acres of land which is under a fine state of cultivation making a desirable home in a community noted for its sobriety, peaceable and industrious people. He took an active interest in helping, encouraging and sustaining the public schools, churches and farmer's organizations, and took a keen interest in the main issues of the day.

On the 19th of Oct., 1875, his wife died and on Apr. 29, 1877, he was married to Mrs. Sarah Rowe. His P. O. address is Pasturefield, Ill.

AMANDA E. BARNES, first wife of Abraham Barnes, was the daughter of Joshua and Maria Elizabeth (Nunemacher) Woliston ; was married to Abraham Barnes Oct. 2, 1856 ; died Oct. 19, 1875. Their children were Philip W., Otto H. and Jay J.

SARAH E. BARNES, daughter of Joshua and Maria E. Wooliston, was married to Abraham Barnes Apr. 29, 1877.

PHILIP W. BARNES.

PHILIP W. BARNES. oldest son of Abraham Barnes, was born near Springfield. Ohio, July 17, 1858: moved from Springfield, Ohio, to near Sumner. Ill., March. 1863: resided with his father on the farm until 1876 when he entered the Olney High School at Olney, Ill., and graduated from same in June, 1879: entered the law school of the Illinois Wesleyan University at Bloomington, Illinois, and graduated in June, 1881, receiving the degree of Bachelor of Laws; was licensed by the Supreme Court of Illinois to practice law; was member of the law firm of Snyder & Barnes from 1881 to 1887 and from 1887 to the present time a member of the law firm of Gee & Barnes of Lawrenceville, Illinois. He was elected County Judge in 1882, reelected in 1886 and served until 1890. In 1887 he entered in Bank business with J. W. McCleave. firm being McCleave & Barnes and known as the "Lawrenceville Bank", continued until 1887, when they sold, since which time the late firm have formed the 1st National Bank of Lawrenceville, Illinois. with Philip W. Barnes as President.

Philip W. Barnes was the Chairman of

the Republican Congressional Committee
of his district from 1886 to 1898; was a
member of the Republican State Committee of his state from 1898 to 1900; was a
delegate to the National Convention at
Minneapolis, Minn., in the year 1892, and
was elected Representative for 45th Sena-
torial district at the November election in
1900.

OTTO H. BARNES, second son of Abraham
Barnes, was born near Springfield, Ohio,
Aug. 10, 1860, and moved with his parents
to Ill. in 1862. He attended the country
school and worked on the farm until 17
when he attended the Olney High School
graduating from there June 6, 1881. After
teaching school one winter he entered the
wholesale drug store of the Richardson
Drug Co., St. Louis, Mo. He remained here
two years and then, after spending several
weeks south, went to Kansas City, Mo.,
and engaged in the retail drug business as
partner of the firm of R. M. Godfrey & Co.
After five years at this place he located at
Salt Lake City, Utah, and engaged in the
Real Estate and Brick business under the
firm name of the Enterprise Brick Co. with

OTTO H. BARNES.

the capacity of 30,000 per day. Because of failing health he returned to his father's farm in the year 1896 where he has since been engaged in farming and stock raising. He was married Nov. 14, 1900, to Miss Mary Fee who lived on an adjoining farm in his own neighborhood. They have one son,

OTTO WARREN BARNES, born Jan 30, 1902.

JAY JUDD BARNES, youngest son of Abraham and Amanda E. Barnes, was born near Sumner, Lawrence Co., Ill., Jan. 26, 1870. He lived with his father on the farm attending the district school until seventeen years old when he attended the High School at Olney, Ill. He then attended college at Danville, Ind. He was a diligent student; a fine writer and composer, leading his class in literary work.

In 1892 he engaged in the brick business with his brother, Otto H. Barnes, at Salt Lake City, Utah, and later in the stock business. He died at Nephi, Utah, Nov. 6, 1896.

ALVA BARNES.

ALVA BARNES, fourth son of Silas Barnes, Sr., was born in West Stockbridge, Berkshire Co., Mass., Dec. 27, 1797; married Catherine Boughton; moved to the town of West Stockbridge, Mass.; was a farmer by occupation; a member of the church, and an industrious, public spirited citizen. He was killed Sep. 3, 1838, by a limb while cutting a bee tree. There were born to them three sons and two daughters, viz.: Cyrus Wm., Laura Ann, Charles H., George and Mary.

Cyrus Wm. Barnes and Family.

CYRUS WM. BARNES, oldest son of Alva and Catherine Barnes, was born in West Stockbridge, Berkshire Co., Mass., May 4, 1821; Married Naomi Hewins of West Stockbridge, Mass.; moved to West Stockbridge Center, where his wife died Dec., 1849. They had one daughter, Fannie Catherine. He married Ellen A. Munn July 4, 1861; moved to Housatonic, Mass., where he lived until his death. There were born to them two children, Lina and Perley. He

CYRUS WM. AND ELLEN A BARNES.

was a farmer by occupation ; died at Housatonic, Mass., March 19, 1898.

ELLEN AUGUSTA BARNES, second wife of Cyrus Wm. Barnes, was born at New Marlborough, Mass., Nov. 10, 1836 ; died Oct. 24, 1901. Her father, Israel W. Munn, was born at Palmyra, N. Y., Nov. 18, 1787 ; married Luna Benedict Sep. 29, 1819 ; was a captain in the war of 1812 ; died Sep. 8, 1874.

FANNIE C. BARNES, daughter of Cyrus W. and Naomi H. Barnes, was born at West Stockbridge, Mass., Dec. 5, 1848 ; went to Hartford, Conn., in 1872, to take care of Mrs. Geo. Gilbert and her daughter who had the consumption. She still resides with the same family at 67 Willard St., Hartford, Conn. ; is a dress-maker by occupation.

LINA N. BARNES, daughter of Cyrus Wm. and Ellen A. Barnes, was born at West Stockbridge, Mass., Oct. 10, 1863 ; resides at Housatonic, Mass.

PERLEY A. BARNES, son of Cyrus Wm. and Ellen A. Barnes, was born at West Stockbridge, Mass., March, 1868 ; is a weaver in the Monument Mills at Housatonic, Mass.

Arvine and Laura A. Heath and Family.

ARVINE HEATH, son of Amos Heath, was born at Tyringham, Berkshire Co., Mass., Aug. 30, 1818; has been an industrious, temperate man ; is a farmer by occupation ; is strong and vigorous in mind and body, at the age of eighty four ; resides at Breedsville, Van Buren Co., Mich.

LAURA ANN HEATH, oldest daughter of Alva Barnes, was born in West Stockbridge, Berkshire Co., Mass., May 22, 1821; died at Arlington, Van Buren Co., Mich., May 20, 1886. She was married to Arvine Heath Jan. 1, 1844. There were born to them two children, Frances Alwilda and George R.

Frances A. Scrimger and Family.

Frances Alwilda Scrimger, daughter of Arvine and Laura A. Heath, was born at Tyringham, Berkshire Co., Mass., Feb. 2, 1845; moved to Mich.; married Alfred W. Scrimger. Their family consisted of four children, as follows : Mary, Alsena J., Cora Ann and Amos J.

She died May 25, 1879. He moved to Frost Tp., Clare Co., Mich., in 1887.

MARY SCRIMGER was born Dec. 20, 1866 ; was a devoted christian ; died Apr. 25, 1878.

OLIVER N. KING, son of Oliver and Dina King, was born at Moorestown, N. Y., June 21, 1869 ; is a dealer in cedar timber, dry goods, groceries and general merchandise at Houghton Lake, Mich. ; is a notary public and holds several township and county offices ; married Alsena J. Scrimger.

ALSENA J. KING, daughter of Alfred W. and Frances A. Scrimger, was born March 31, 1870 ; was married to Oliver N. King in Clare Co., Mich., March 31, 1889. They have three children, as follows :

ROY N. KING was born in Clare Co., Mich., June 13, 1891.

FRANCES G. KING was born in Clare Co., Mich., Oct. 30, 1894.

MARY ALSENA KING was born at Houghton Lake, Mich., Apr. 13, 1901.

Their P. O. address is Houghton Lake, Mich.

Reuben D. Gleason, son of Lyman Gleason, was born in the state of New York Oct. 23, 1870; married Cora Ann Gleason.

Cora Ann Gleason, daughter of Alfred W. and Frances A. Scrimger, was born in Arlington Tp., Van Buren Co., Mich., Feb. 2, 1874; moved to Frost Tp., Clare Co., Mich.; is a faithful christian worker in the M. E. Church. She was married to Reuben Dwight Gleason, Feb. 22, 1891. They have three children, as follows:

Louise S. Gleason, born Nov. 14, 1891.

Minnie Gleason, born Jan. 6, 1894.

Wm. Daniel Gleason, born March 12, 1899. Their P. O. address is Harrison, Clare Co., Mich.

———

Amos J. Scrimger, son of Alfred W. and Frances A. Scrimger, was born Oct. 29, 1876; resides in Frost Tp., Clare Co., Mich; is a farmer by occupation; was married July 4, 1901, at Harrison, Mich., to Sarah E. Klinger. They are enterprising and industrious; much interested in moral and religious work; have one child, Pansy.

Pansy Scrimger was born May 4, 1902.

George R. Heath and Family.

GEORGE R. HEATH, son of Arvine and Laura A. Heath, was born at West Stockbridge, Berkshire Co., Mass., Oct. 20, 1847; is a farmer by occupation; P. O. is Breedsville, Mich.

LOTTIE E. YORK was born in Saratoga Co., N. Y., Oct. 2, 1848.

George R. Heath and Lottie E. York were married at Arlington, Van Buren Co. Mich., Nov. 5, 1868. They had two children, L. Roy and Mabel.

L. ROY HEATH, son of George R. Heath, was born at Arlington, Van Buren Co., Mich., July 2, 1872. He married Miss ORA WILLIAMS.

MABEL HEATH LEATHERS, daughter of George R. Heath, was born at Arlington, Van Buren Co., Mich., Jan. 22, 1878; married Henry Leathers. They live in Columbia Township, Van Buren Co., Mich.; have one daughter, Gladys.

GLADYS LEATHERS was born July 25, 1896.

CHARLES H. BARNES.

MRS. CHARLES H. BARNES.

Charles H. Barnes and Family.

CHARLES H. BARNES, son of Alva Barnes, was born at West Stockbridge, Mass., Apr. 12, 1830; died at Homer, Mich., Nov. 16, 1894.

HARRIET M. BARNES, daughter of Martin W. Osborn, was born at Austerlitz, Columbia Co., N. Y., May 29, 1833.

Charles H. Barnes and Harriet M. Osborn were married March 31, 1853, at Austerlitz, N. Y., by Rev. James J. Utley of the first Congregational Church of Green River, N. Y.; moved on a farm at West Stockbridge Center; lived there three years and then moved to West Stockbridge Village where he was in the employ of the Housatonic R. R. Co., as freight agent, until he enlisted in the army Aug. 30, 1862. He was mustered into the 49th Reg. Mass. Vol.; was in the battles of Plains Store (Baton Rouge), Vicksburg and Port Hudson. At the latter place he received a sun stroke which, with other disabilities contracted in the army, caused him to be an invalid for life, and finally caused his death after long years of patient suffering.   His young wife, with patriotic devotion, cheerfully took upon herself the burden and care of the family.

In March, 1865, they moved to Homer, Mich., where, for thirty years, she carried on a dress-making establishment, sometimes employing from ten to twelve sewing girls. Her home is at Corner of Main and Hillsdale St., Homer, Mich. There were born to them four daughters, as follows: Ida Maria, Elizabeth Anna, Lillie Harriet and Mary Catherine.

IDA M. ARTHUR, daughter of Charles H. and Harriet M. Barnes, was born at Austerlitz, Columbia Co., N. Y., July 5, 1854; married P. Arthur; resides at 668 Dorr St., Toledo, O.

ELIZABETH A. OSBORN, daughter of Charles H. and Harriet M. Barnes, was born at West Stockbridge, Mass., June 10, 1859; married B. R. Osborn. They have two children, as follows:

CLARA E. OSBORN, born May 18, 1883, at Tekonsha, Mich.

CHARLES RUFUS OSBORN, born June 10, 1890, at Tekonsha, Mich.

They reside at Tekonsha, Mich.

Residence of CHARLES H. BARNES, Homer, Mich

LILLIE H. SNIDER, daughter of Charles H. and Harriet M. Barnes, was born at Austerlitz, Columbia Co., N. Y., May 27, 1862 ; married Alonzo Snider. They have four children, all born at Homer, Mich., as follows :

UNA A. SNIDER, born Jan. 9, 1887.

IDA E. SNIDER, born Feb. 15, 1889.

LOUISA L. SNIDER, born Sep. 24, 1891.

OLIN B. SNIDER, born March 11, 1897.

They reside at Homer, Mich.

MARY C. MARZOLF, daughter of Charles H. and Harriet M. Barnes, was born at Homer, Mich., Jan. 16, 1868 ; married Alexander Marzolf. They reside at Toledo, O. ; have one son,

RONALD B. MARZOLF, born at Albion, Mich., Dec. 9, 1893.

John H. and Mary Barnes Fairfield.

JOHN H. FAIRFIELD was born at Pittsfield, Mass., Nov. 6, 1828 ; married Mary Barnes ; resides at Richmond, Mass.

MARY B. FAIRFIELD, wife of John H. Fairfield, was the youngest daughter of Alva

Barnes. She was born at West Stockbridge, Mass., Oct. 8, 1836, and died at Richmond, Mass., Feb. 26, 1902. They had two children, Frances and John H.

——

Frank D. Smith, son of Henry C. Smith, was born at Feeding Hills, Mass., Sep. 20, 1864; married Frances Fairfield; P. O. address is Westfield, Mass.

Frances F. Smith, wife of Frank D. Smith and daughter of John H. and Mary Fairfield, was born at Richmond, Mass., May 16, 1861, and died at Westfield, Mass., March 5, 1888. They had one daughter, Frances E. Smith, who was born at Westfield, Mass., Feb. 28, 1888, and resides at Richmond, Mass.

———

John H. Fairfield, Jr., son of John H. and Mary Barnes Fairfield, was born at Richmond, Mass., Aug. 6, 1871; married Blanche L. Bradley; resides at Richmond, Mass.; is engaged at farming; P. O. address is Pittsfield, Mass., R. F. D.

Blanche L. Fairfield, wife of John H. Fairfield, Jr. and daughter of Luther W. and Mary C. Bradley, was born at West

Stockbridge, Mass., July 14, 1872.

Her grandmother Bradley was Lucy M. Barnes, the youngest daughter, and her grandmother Reed was Charlotte Barnes, the third daughter of Silas Barnes, Sr.

ANNA BARNES, oldest daughter of Silas Barnes, born May 8, 1793, was married twice; first time to Timothy Brown, second time to Mr. Shaw.

LOUISA BARNES, second daughter of Silas Barnes. Sr., was born Sep. 11, 1795; died May 26, 1796.

CHARLES AND CHARLOTTE BARNES REED.

CHARLES REED, born June 9, 1801, and CHARLOTTE BARNES, third daughter of Silas Barnes, Sr., born Nov. 2, 1802, resided at West Stockbridge, Mass., from the time of birth until their death. Charlotte died July 27, 1867; Charles died May 19, 1881. They were married at Canaan, N. Y., by Elder Hall, Sep. 9, 1822. Nine children were born to them, as follows:

CHARLES ARTEMAS, born Jan. 1, 1824, died Oct. 1, 1826.

CHARLOTTE ARTEMECIA, born Feb. 14, 1826, died Oct. 26, 1826.

BETSEY ANNA, born Nov. 24, 1827, died at Springfield, Mass., Feb. 13, 1893.

CHARLES DEODATUS, born March 18, 1831, was a soldier in the War of the Rebellion, was killed in 1864.

SILAS E., born May 12, 1834, died at Breedsville, Mich., Apr. 7, 1857.

TIMOTHY BROWN, born Dec. 11, 1836, died at West Stockbridge, Mass. March 30, 1899.

CHARLOTTE AMY, born Nov. 30, 1840, died Aug. 6, 1842.

MARY CELINA, born Sep. 20, 1843, married Luther Wm. Bradley. They have a daughter, Blanche, who married John H. Fairfield, Jr.

CHARLOTTE EMILY, born Dec. 29, 1847.

ELIHU S. AND LUCY M. BRADLEY.

LUCY MARIAH BRADLEY, youngest daughter of Silas Barnes, Sr., was born in West Stockbridge, Mass., Nov. 19, 1808; was married to Elihu S. Bradley Apr. 6, 1831. They had three children, as follows:

JUDSON, born Jan. 19, 1835.

LUTHER WM., born Jan. 10, 1841.

THEODORET J., born Feb. 24, 1843.

Judson Bradley married Ellen M. Kingsley, Feb. 20, 1873; had two children as follows;

OLIVE B., born Nov. 7, 1877.

LUCY M., born June 9, 1880.

Luther Wm. Bradley married Mary C. Reed, daughter of Charles and Charlotte Barnes Reed, Nov. 30, 1865; reside at West Stockbridge, Mass.; have had six children,

DWIGHT, born July 27, 1867.

CHARLOTTE L., born Sep. 14, 1869.

BLANCHE L., born July 14, 1872.

ANNA J., born June 15, 1874.

AMY L. born Feb. 17, 1877.

ETHEL G. born Nov. 3, 1885.

NOTES.

1. LYDIA L. KIMBALL, oldest daughter of W. H. and Mary M. Canfield, was married in Feb., 1878, to Alonzo D. Struble of Lyons, Mich.: was married again in Nov., 1898, to Stephen H. Kimball of Lyons, Mich.

ELMA L. KIMBALL, youngest daughter of W. H. and Mary M. Canfield, was married Apr. 2, 1886, to Wm. H. Kimball of Lyons, Mich. Mr. Kimball died Feb. 10, 1902.

This record was not received in time to put where it belongs on page 27.

CHAPTER III.

TIMOTHY BARNES AND HIS DESCENDANTS.

TIMOTHY BARNES, Jr., third son of Timothy Barnes, Sr., was born in Southington, Conn., Apr. 9, 1769; moved with his father to West Stockbridge, Mass., in 1778; was married twice. His first wife was Betsey Johnson, his second wife was Polly Webb. They lived at Alford, Mass.; had one son, Abraham.

ABRAHAM BARNES.

ABRAHAM BARNES, son of Timothy Barnes, Jr., was born at Alford, Mass., Sep. 15, 1790. He was enterprising and industrious, a faithful Christian, highly esteemed by all who knew him.

SALLY BASSET was born May 24, 1783.

Abraham Barnes and Sally Basset were married Sep. 22, 1814; lived at Alford, Mass.; had five children, Mary, Harvey A., Amos, Betsey and Timothy.

MARY BARNES was born Nov. 24, 1816.

HARVEY A. BARNES, born Feb. 21, 1819, died Sep. 3, 1820.

AMOS BARNES, born Dec. 26, 1821, had three children, Ensign, Harvey and Josephine. Ensign resides at Hattiesburg, Miss.

BETSEY BARNES was born Feb. 7, 1823.

Timothy Barnes and Family.

TIMOTHY BARNES, youngest son of Abraham Barnes, was born Feb. 7, 1823.

RHODA BILLS was born Jan. 16, 1827; was married to Timothy Barnes in 1846. They reside at North Egremont, Mass. Their children were Mary J., William, Frances E. and Charlotte.

MARY J., born Feb. 14, 1847, married Mr. Rice; resides at Ashley Falls, Mass.

WILLIAM, born June 27, 1849, is dead.

FRANCES E., born Dec. 11, 1852, married Mr. Taylor; resides at Gt. Barrington, Mass.; has three children, as follows:

ODA A., born Jan. 15, 1872; died Feb. 22, 1879.

THEODORE D., born at Colchester, Conn., Oct. 7, 1877; resides at San Francisco, Cal.

Mrs. PARMELEE, born Apr. 19, 1881, resides at Gt. Barrington, Mass.

CHAPTER IV.

ELISHA BARNES AND HIS DESCENDANTS.

ELISHA BARNES, fourth son, of Timothy Barnes, was born in Southington, Conn., March 11, 1771; went with his father to West Stockbridge, Mass.; married Vilate Ford March 3, 1796; died Nov. 19, 1872,

VILATE F. BARNES, wife of Elisha Barnes, born in June, 1775, died Dec. 13, 1848.

They had a family of seven children, as follows: Erastus, Asahel, Betsey, Elisha Munson, Seth Austin, Thomas Wm. and Nancy Vilate, all born in West Stockbridge, Berkshire Co., Mass.

Elisha Barnes made the following statement when he was ninety years old:

"Timothy Barnes moved from Southington(which once belonged to Farmington), Conn., to West Stockbridge, Mass., June 8, 1878; had a brother Lemuel, a brother Phinehas and a sister Mary who married a Mr. Mills."

ERASTUS BARNES.

ERASTUS BARNES, oldest son of Elisha Barnes Sr., was born in West Stockbridge, Berkshire Co, Mass., Jan. 2, 1797; was a carpenter by trade; married Nancy Crampton; moved to Binghamton, N. Y., in 1881 where they resided until their death. He died Aug. 6, 1856, and she died Sep. 3, 1881.

There were born to them four sons and one daughter, as follows: Erastus Benjamin, Elisha Asahel, Morgan L., Elmore P. and Nancy.

Erastus Benjamin Barnes and Family.

ERASTUS B. BARNES, first son of Erastus Barnes, born Apr. 23, 1822, died in 1856. He was a carpenter by trade, lived and died at Binghamton, N. Y.; had two children, William Erastus and Nellie.

WILLIAM E. BARNES, born Aug. 29, 1857, spent the early part of his life at Binghamton, N. Y.; was employed in the Susquehanna Valley Bank at that place; is now cashier of the Western Branch of the Security Mutual Life Insurance Association at

Minneapolis, Minn.

MARY MORSE BARNES, daughter of Frederick A. Thompson, was born Apr. 11, 1863; was married to William E. Barnes Apr. 8, 1886. There were born to them three children, as follows:

MARGARET CONTENT BARNES, born Jan. 1, 1887.

HELEN AGNES BARNES, born March 8, 1891.

MURRAY ERASTUS BARNES, born May 5, 1893, died July 6, 1893.

NELLIE BARNES BROCK, daughter of Erastus B. Barnes, married Rev. George A. Brock.

ELISHA ASAHEL BARNES, second son of Erastus Barnes, born Apr. 9, 1825, died in 1828.

Morgan L. Barnes.

MORGAN L. BARNES, third son of Erastus Barnes, was born at West Stockbridge, Mass., June 21, 1827; died at Binghamton, N. Y., Nov. 14, 1895.

SARAH M. BARNES, daughter of Isaac A. Finny, was born at Ghent, Columbia Co., N. Y., July 29, 1829; is proprietress of the Oak Street Greenhouses, 124 Oak Street, Binghamton, N. Y.

Morgan L. Barnes and Sarah M. Finny were married May 28, 1856. They have resided in Binghamton the most of the time for over forty years. He was a grocer and insurance agent the most of his life. They were members and loyal supporters of the West Presbyterian church.

The following notice is copied from a Binghamton paper dated Nov. 16, 1895:

"After months of failing health Morgan L. Barnes passed peacefully away Thursday night at eleven o'clock, in the sixty-ninth year of his age. Mr. Barnes was one of Binghamton's most highly esteemed citizens. He had resided here since his boyhood, with the exception of four years spent in Denver, Col., from 1879 to 1883. He was one of the founders of the West Presbyterian church in this city, and held the office of ruling elder in the church from the day of its organization in his house on Oak street nearly twenty-three years ago."

ELMORE P. BARNES, fourth son of Erastus Barnes, born July 22, 1832, died in 1833.

NANCY SMITH, daughter of Erastus Barnes, is living at Binghamton, N. Y.

OSCAR E. BARNEY. P 133

On page 141 is his picture taken earlier in life.

ASAHEL BARNES, second son of Elisha Barnes, born Oct. 4, 1800, died Apr. 1, 1823.

BETSEY B. CRAMPTON, daughter of Elisha Barnes, born Nov. 5, 1802, married Horace Crampton Jan. 17, 1821 ; moved to Amboy, Lee Co., Ill., about 1867 ; died at Amboy, Ill., about 1890.

ELISHA MUNSON BARNES.

ELISHA M. BARNES, third son of Elisha Barnes, born in West Stockbridge, Mass., died Dec. 2, 1804. He married Marinda Bristol. There were born to them four sons and three daughters, as follows : Oscar Evander, Edward Everett, Hannah V., Elizabeth, Lester, Martha Jane and Wheaton Prindle.

Oscar Evander Barnes and Family.

OSCAR E. BARNES, first son of Elisha M. Barnes, was born in West Stockbridge, Mass., Feb. 23, 1828 ; married Mary E. Patrick, and lived in West Stockbridge until 1854 when they moved to Napoleon, Henry Co., O., by the way of Toledo, O. ; left West Stockbridge the last of April and arrived at Napoleon, on a packet from Toledo, on

May 3, 1854. He has lived nearly all of the time since 1854 at Napoleon; has served Henry Co. in the official capacity of Deputy Sheriff four years, Sheriff two terms, Clerk of Common Pleas and District Court fifteen years, and the last four years was health officer for the city of Napoleon.
He died Nov. 20, 1902.

MARY ELIZABETH BARNES, daughter of Trowbridge Patrick, was born at Chatham, N. Y., Apr. 2, 1831; married Oscar E. Barnes; died at Napoleon, O., Sep. 13, 1858. They had one son, Elbert Trowbridge.

ELIZABETH L. BARNES, second wife of Oscar E. Barnes, and daughter of John Orcutt, was born in Geneseeo, N. Y., March 8, 1838; died at Napoleon, O., March 19, 1890. They had one daughter, Mary Elizabeth.

ELBERT T. BARNES, son of Oscar E. and Mary E. Barnes, was born in West Stockbridge, Mass., March 21, 1851; went to Napoleon, O., in 1854; has been Sheriff of Henry Co., O.; is a farmer; resides in Henry Co.; P. O. address is Napoleon, O.

KATHERYN BARNES, wife of Elbert T. Barnes, was born at Napoleon, O., Jan. 12,

1851. Their family consists of two sons and one daughter, as follows:

NELLIE M. BARNES, born Oct. 10, 1874.

OSCAR EDWARD BARNES, born Dec. 7, 1876.

JOHN T. BARNES, born July 27, 1882.

All were born and now reside at Napoleon, Ohio.

MARY ELIZABETH BARNES, daughter of Oscar E. and Elizabeth Barnes, was born at Napoleon, O., Sep. 23, 1865: has been a teacher in the Union School at Napoleon for the last seventeen years. For several years, during vacation, she has lectured on primary work in different parts of the state, the last two years at Mt. Union College, Alliance, Stark Co., Ohio.

Her P. O. address is Napoleon, Ohio.

EDWARD EVERETT BARNES, second son of Elisha Munson Barnes, born at West Stockbridge, Mass., Feb. 6, 1831, has no children: P. O. address is Gt. Barrington, Mass.

HANNAH V. BARNES, daughter of Elisha M. Barnes, born March 26, 1833, is dead.

ELIZABETH WOOD, second daughter of Elisha M. Barnes, born Aug. 5, 1835, married John A. Wood Jan. 1, 1855. They live at 106 Montague St., Brooklyn, N. Y.; had two daughters, as follows:

NELLIE B., born at Westfield, N. Y., Feb. 25, 1860, married Edward F. Giddings Feb. 16, 1879.

CARRIE P., born July 18, 1866, died Aug. 19, 1879.

LESTER BARNES, third son of Elisha M. Barnes, born Oct. 13, 1837, is dead.

Jay N. and Martha J. Preston and Family.

JAY N. PRESTON, son of Judd M. Preston, was born at East Chatham, N. Y., Aug. 2, 1834.

MARTHA J. PRESTON, youngest daughter of Elisha M. Barnes, was born at Stockbridge, Mass., Oct. 18, 1839; married Jay N. Preston Apr. 21, 1856. They reside at East Chatham N. Y.; had six children, as follows: Mary E., Carrie L., Nellie E., Ada L., William B. and Henry J.

W. J. KIRBY was born at East Chatham, N. Y., Nov. 25, 1858.

MARY E. KIRBY, daughter of Jay N. and Martha J. Preston, born at East Chatham, N. Y., March 22, 1859, married W. J. Kirby in 1881. They reside at East Chatham, N. Y.; have one daughter, Nellie M.

NELLIE M. KIRBY was born at East Chatham, N. Y., Jan. 27, 1882.

CHARLES A. HAMILTON, born in Canaan, N. Y., March 24, 1859, married Carrie L. Preston.

CARRIE L. HAMILTON, daughter of Jay N. and Martha J. Preston, born at East Chatham, N. Y., Jan. 4, 1861, married C. A. Hamilton May 19, 1881. They have two children as follows:

C. HAROLD HAMILTON, born at Brooklyn, N. Y., Sep. 9, 1884.

KENNETH P. HAMILTON, born at Fairmount, N. J., Dec. 31, 1886.

H. SANFORD MEAD was born at Fishkill, N. Y., July 16, 1865.

NELLIE E. MEAD, daughter of Jay N. and Martha J. Preston, born at East Chatham, N. Y., Sep. 2, 1866, married H. Sanford Mead Sep. 28, 1888.

W. C. ORCHARD, born at London, England, Nov. 30, 1863, married Ada L. Preston.

ADA L. ORCHARD, daughter of Jay N. and

Martha J. Preston, born at East Chatham, N. Y., Sep. 15, 1869, married W. C. Orchard Dec. 4, 1890. They have three children, as follows :

FRED P. ORCHARD was born at Lenox, Mass., Oct. 10, 1891.

MARJORIE E. ORCHARD was born at Lenox, Mass., Nov. 13, 1894.

W. SANFORD ORCHARD was born at New York City Sep. 21, 1897.

WM. B. PRESTON, son of Jay N. and M. J. Preston, born at East Chatham, N. Y., Nov. 20, 1874, married Hattie B. Adams. She was born Apr. 6, 1874.

HENRY J. PRESTON, born Dec. 13, 1875, died Jan 25, 1881.

WHEATON P. BARNES, fourth son of Elisha M. Barnes was born in Stockbridge, Mass., Aug. 23, 1846 ; was a Union soldier in the Civil War; married Olive L., daughter of Elnathan and Elizabeth Barnes, Dec. 25, 1871. She was born Oct. 15, 1850, and died at Amboy, Ill., Nov. 10, 1898. He moved to Amboy, Lee Co., Ill., Apr. 12, 1891 ; married Olive G. Hague Oct. 30, 1900, at Napoleon, Henry Co., O. ; is a grain dealer ; resides at Amboy, Ill.

SETH AUSTIN BARNES.

SETH AUSTIN BARNES, fourth son of Elisha Barnes, born in West Stockbridge, Mass., June 28, 1808, was a farmer by occupation, and owned a good farm at Williamsville. (West Stockbridge) Berkshire Co., Mass., where he lived and died. In the latter part of his life he was engaged in the grocery business. He married Caroline H. Williams of Stockbridge, Mass. They had two children, Ellen E. and William H. He died March 23, 1891.

ELLEN E. BARNES. born Oct. 15, 1835, died Apr. 15, 1870. She lived and died at the old home with her father.

William H. Barnes and Family.

WILLIAM H. BARNES, son of Seth Austin Barnes, born in West Stockbridge, Mass., Jan. 28, 1838, was a soldier in the War of the Rebellion, enlisted as a private in Co. C, 37th Mass. Reg.; served three years; was wounded in the battle of the Wilderness. He was a public spirited man, much interested in township and county affairs;

was justice of the peace a number of years, and served as assessor several terms; was a civil engineer and in the different branches of his business was brought in contact with the best and most influential citizens. He was a man of sound judgment and strict integrity, a member and a deacon of the Congregational church at Housatonic, Mass. He died at his home July 31, 1901. He married Martha French.

MARTHA F. BARNES, born in West Stockbridge, Mass., Nov. 28, 1836, was married to Wm. H. Barnes May 2, 1862. They lived in West Stockbridge on the old farm that has been owned and occupied by the Barnes people about one hundred and twenty years, at a place now called Williamsville, about one mile west of Housatonic, Mass. Their children are Florence A. and Jay Preston.

FLORENCE A. SEDGWICK, daughter of William H. and Martha F. Barnes, born in West Stockbridge, Mass., March 21, 1868, married Edward C. Sedgwick May 23, 1900.

EDWARD C. SEDGWICK, born at Lenox, Mass., June 25, 1865, married Florence A. Barnes. He is a Congregational clergyman;

was ordained at Curtisville, Mass.

They have one daughter, Mary. They reside at Lenox, Mass.

MARY SEDGWICK was born in Curtisville, Mass., Sep. 28, 1901.

JAY PRESTON BARNES, son of William H. and Martha F. Barnes, was born in West Stockbridge, Mass., Aug. 9, 1869. He graduated from the Great Barrington High school, and took a special course in Civil Engineering in Cornell University. He is a civil engineer; resides at 46 Benton Terrace, Pittsfield, Mass. He married Henrietta Dutton, of Waterbury, Conn. They have three children, as follows:

HAROLD DUTTON BARNES, born Sep. 28, 1895.

MARGARET BARNES, born Oct. 10, 1899.

WILLIAM HAMILTON BARNES, born March 6, 1903. All were born at Pittsfield, Mass.

THOMAS WM. BARNES.

THOMAS WM. BARNES.

THOMAS WM. BARNES, fifth son of Elisha Barnes, was born in West Stockbridge, Mass., Feb. 9, 1811. He received a good education ; was an influential political worker in the Republican party ; was a member of the State legislature, representing the West Stockbridge district, in 1847—48. He was engaged in farming and milling ; owned a large farm and was a member of the firm of Platt & Barnes, large manufacturers of Platt's Patent Buckwheat Flour, Wheat Flour and Feed.

He died in West Stockbridge, Mass., Jan. 22, 1885.

ZILPHA ARNOLD BARNES and Thomas Wm. Barnes were married Oct. 26, 1841. They resided at Williamsville, in West Stockbridge, Mass.; had two children, Erwin F. and Charles D. Barnes.

She died Dec. 27, 1858.

EMELINE COLBOURN BARNES, second wife of Thomas Wm. Barnes, born near Chatham, N. Y., March 16, 1836, was married to Thomas Wm. Barnes Apr. 26, 1876.

ERWIN F. BARNES.

Erwin F. Barnes and Family.

ERWIN FRANK BARNES, son of Thomas W.
and Zilpha A. Barnes, was born in West
Stockbridge, Mass., March 14, 1846. After
attending the public schools of West Stockbridge, he received a thorough education in
the following institutions of learning :

The Hudson River Institute at Claverack,
N. Y., the South Berkshire Institute at
New Marlborough, Mass., and Prof. Marshall Warner's private school at Stockbridge, Mass.

After leaving school he spent one year as
clerk at Housatonic, Mass. In 1872 he entered the employ of Platt, Barnes & Co., and
in 1875 became a member of the firm. In
1880 Mr. Pomeroy went out of the business,
in 1885 Thomas Wm. Barnes died, and in
1892 Mr. E. F. Barnes bought out his partner, Mr. Charles S. Platt ; and since that
time he has carried on the milling business
alone. He has a good mill, thoroughly
equipped, supplied with water power of
thirty feet head. Besides general
milling, his chief business and his spec-
ialty is the manufacture of self-raising

buckwheat flour. His facilities for the manufacture of this popular article include a
patent hulling-machine of great economic
value in the industry. He carries on his
business intelligently and conservatively
and with certain though not extravagant
profits.

He is a Republican in politics ,and in 1895
represented, in the Mass. General Court,
the Sixth Berkshire Representative District. In 1877 he received the appointment
of postmaster at Rock Dale Mills, and has
held the office ever since. He has held the
office of selectman in the town of West
Stockbridge for four consecutive years.

He married Miss Augusta Joyner.

AUGUSTA M .BARNES, daughter of John M.
and Fanny B. Joyner, born Sep. 11, 1848,
was married to Erwin F. Barnes Jan. 14,
1874. There were born to them four children, as follows :

CHARLES DWIGHT BARNES, born June 15,
1881, a graduate of the Searles High School
of Great Barrington, Mass., is bookkeeper
in his father's office at Rock Dale Mills.

MIRIAM ELIZABETH BARNES, born March
30, 1883.

Rock Dale Mills, Erwin F. Barnes Proprietor.

LENA AUGUSTA BARNES, born May 13, 1885.

THOMAS WILLIAM BARNES, born May 10, 1887.

CHARLES DWIGHT BARNES, son of Thomas William Barnes, born Aug. 28, 1848, was killed by a horse running away Sep. 4, 1858.

BETSEY BARNES CRAMPTON.

BETSEY B. CRAMPTON, oldest daughter of Elisha Barnes, born Nov. 5, 1802, married Horace Crampton Jan. 17, 1821; moved to Amboy, Lee Co., Ill., about 1867; died at Amboy, Ill., about 1860.

NANCY V. SEELEY.

NANCY V. SEELEY, youngest daughter of Elisha Barnes, was born in West Stockbridge, Mass., Sep. 5, 1814, and died at Lenox, Mass., May 22, 1889.

ERASTUS MILES SEELEY was born in Gt. Barrington, Mass., Oct. 16, 1814; was a blacksmith by trade; married Nancy Violet Barnes; died at Housatonic, Mass., Apr. 15, 1894.   They had four children,

Ann Eliza, Alice Louise, Gertrude M. and Wallace E.

Ann Eliza Smith and Family.

Ann Eliza Smith, oldest daughter of E. M. and Nancy V. Seeley, was born at West Stockbridge, Mass., Aug. 5, 1836 : married D. Newton Smith at Lenox, Mass., Feb. 24, 1855 ; resides at Pittsfield, Mass. ; had six children, as follows : Nettie L., Grace, Ellery D., Harry S., Edward and Gertrude L. Nettie and Edward are dead.

Grace married Clark N. Phelps of Housatonic in Feb., 1887. Mr. Phelps is dead and she lives at Buffalo, N. Y.

Ellery D. married Nellie Warner of Housatonic. They live at Gt. Barrington, Mass.

Harry S. married Lillian L. Tucker of Lenox, Mass. They live at Gt. Barrington, Mass.

Gertrude L. lives with her mother at Pittsfield, Mass.

Alice L. Ross and Family.

Alice L. Ross, daughter of E. Miles and Nancy V. Seeley, was born at Alford,

Mass., Apr. 15, 1843 ; married Joseph S. Ross, of Lenox, in April, 1861 ; has two sons, Charles S. and Leon A.

CHARLES S. married Nellie E. Hill, Pittsfield, Mass., Nov. 17, 1887 ; had four children. Alice G., Henry(dead), Grace C. and Wallace M.

LEON A. married Lillion Minot of Bridgeport, Conn., Dec. 30, 1897 ; has one son, Leon Alerton ; all live at Gt. Barrington.

GERTRUDE M. SEELEY, daughter of E. M. and Nancy V. Seeley, born in Stockbridge, Mass., Jan. 11, 1846, lives in Lenox, Mass.

WALLACE ELISHA SEELEY, son of E. Miles and Nancy V. Seeley, was born in Stockbridge, Mass., Sep. 18, 1855 ; married Mary E. Kilbourne, of Gt. Barrington, Dec. 29. 1887. They have two children, as follows

HAROLD KILBOURN, born Oct. 3, 1888.

LOUISE GERTRUDE, born Dec. 5, 1891.

All live at Housatonic, Mass.

OSCAR E. BARNES. See page 123.

SETH BARNES.

SETH BARNES, fifth son of Timothy Barnes, Jr., was born in Southington, Conn., Feb. 10, 1774; moved with his parents to West Stockbridge, Mass., June 8, 1778; married Mehetabel Baker. They moved to Victor, N. Y., about 1815; had three sons, as follows: Reuben, Elisha and Lemon.

REUBEN BARNES, son of Seth Barnes, was married; moved to Angola, N. Y.; was a carpenter and joiner by trade.

ELISHA BARNES, son of Seth Barnes, married Jerusha Palmer. They resided at Victor, N. Y.

LEMON BARNES, son of Seth Barnes, was married and went to one of the Western states.

CHAPTER V.

ISAAC BARNES AND HIS DESCENDANTS.

ISAAC BARNES, sixth son of Timothy Barnes, Sr., was born in West Stockbridge, Berkshire Co., Mass., June 13, 1778; died at Brighton, N. Y., Dec. 30, 1863.

SARAH FOOTE BARNES was born at Colchester, Conn., Sep. 17, 1779; died at Brighton, N. Y., May 24, 1866.

Isaac Barnes and Sarah Foote were married at West Stockbridge, Mass., by Rev. Oliver Ayers, March 17, 1802; moved to Brighton, Monroe Co., N. Y., in 1814; were economical and industrious, accumulated property and were quite well off before they died. They owned a sawmill, gristmill and three good farms. There were born to them six children, as follows: Miller, Emily, Charles Milo, Mary, Milon D. and Edwin Milton.

MILLER BARNES, first son of Isaac Barnes, born in 1804, married Charlotte Squares; lived and died at Batavia, N. Y.

ISAAC BARNES.

SARAH F. BARNES.

EMILY BARNES WEST.

EMILY BARNES WEST, daughter of Isaac and Sarah Barnes, was born at West Stockbridge. Mass., Aug. 14, 1806, and died at Ridgeway, N. Y., Oct. 27, 1884.

HENRY WEST and Emily Barnes were married and moved to Ridgeway, N. Y. Their children were Miller, Isaac Barnes, Charles Henry and Elisha.

MILLER WEST was married; had no children.

ISAAC BARNES WEST was married; had one son, Charles Henry.
Case.

CHARLES Henry WEST, son of Isaac Barnes West, was married, has two children. They reside at No.39, 1st St., Rochester, N. Y.
Case

CHARLES HENRY WEST, son of Henry and Emily Barnes West, was born about 1840; was a minister, and a student in Oberlin College, at Oberlin, Ohio, when the War of the Rebellion commenced; raised a company of volunteers and enlisted in July, 1862; received a lieutenant's commission; was killed in action at Ream's Station, Va., Aug. 25, 1874.

ELISHA WEST, youngest son of Henry and Emily West, resides at Ridgeway, N. Y.

CHARLES MILO BARNES.

CHARLES MILO BARNES, second son of Isaac and Sarah Barnes, was born in West Stockbridge, Mass., May 5, 1811 ; went to Brighton, N. Y., with his parents when he was three years old. He married Hannah Maria Palmer in 1840 ; went to California in 1849, and was there when San Francisco was burned in 1850 ; returned to New York and was engaged in farming and milling at Brighton ; was justice of the peace twenty four years ; owned a farm and a good grist mill ; was caught by a shaft and killed in the mill at Brighton, N. Y., Dec. 16, 1884.

HANNAH MARIA BARNES, wife of Charles M. Barnes, was born at Stockbridge, Mass., July 11, 1813 ; died at Stockbridge, Mass., Nov. 4, 1885. She was a daughter of Captain Rosswell Palmer who was a sea captain twenty years. He enlisted in the Continental army when he was sixteen years old ; was taken prisoner and put on board the old Jersey Ship in New York Harbor ; had the dropsy and would have died but was taken off by an old Scotch doctor who took pity on him. Within twenty four hours after

CHARLES MILO BARNES.

HANNAH MARIA BARNES.

he was taken off the British sank the ship with all on board.

Charles M. Barnes and Hannah M. Palmer were married in 1840 ; had two children, Charles Palmer and Fannie Maria.

Charles P. Barnes and Family.

CHARLES P. BARNES, son of Charles M. and Hannah M. Barnes, was born at Stockbridge, Berkshire Co., Mass., March 10, 1843 ; owns a farm and a grist mill ; was justice of the peace two terms, and is postmaster at Brighton, N. Y. He married Mary J. Waldron. They have five children, Frank E., Harry P., Clarence W., Charles M. and Bessie M.

MARY J. BARNES, born at Rochester, N. Y., June 28, 1853, was a descendant of Baron Von Waldron who came to this country in an early day. He had a grant of land from the Dutch king situated on Manhattan Island. This claim is now pending, and amounts to millions of dollars.

FRANK ERWIN BARNES, born at Tidioute, Pa., Apr. 25, 1872, married Belle Margaret Pooler.

HARRY PALMER BARNES, born at Brighton, N. Y., Apr. 17, 1874.

CLARENCE WALDRON BARNES, born at Brighton, N. Y., Oct. 13, 1880.

CHARLES MILO and BESSIE MARIA BARNES were twins, born at Brighton, N. Y., Feb. 11, 1885.

They all reside at Brighton, N. Y.

Horace and Fannie M. Strowger.

HORACE BRYAN STROWGER, son of William Strowger, born at Penfield, N. Y., Sep. 4, 1850, is a contractor and builder.

FANNIE MARIA STROWGER, daughter of Charles M. and Hannah M. Barnes, born at Brighton, N. Y., June 9, 1848, was married to Horace B. Strowger at her home in Brighton, N. Y., March 20, 1878. They reside at Brighton, N. Y.; have four children, as follows:

ERNEST PALMER, born March 31, 1879.

FANNIE GRACE, born Feb. 20, 1881.

CHARLES WILLIAM, born Sep. 4, 1883.

JESSIE MARIA, born Dec. 2, 1890.

All were born at Brighton, N. Y.

WILLIAM N. AND MARY E. SHEPARD.

Wm. N. Shepard, born at Chatham, N. Y., Jan. 31, 1805, died Aug. 5, 1885.

Mary Emeline Shepard, daughter of Isaac and Sarah Barnes, born at West Stockbridge, Mass., Oct. 13, 1813, died at Pittsford, N. Y., Dec. 9, 1889.

Wm. Shepard and Mary E. Barnes were married at Brighton, N. Y., Oct. 16, 1838. Their children were Mary Emily, Sarah Florinda, Lucy Kirby. Wm. Miller, Charlotte Louisa, Isaac Barnes and George N.

Geo. N. died young.

Oscar and Mary E. Stoutenburg.

Oscar Stoutenburg, son of Abram Stoutenburg, born at Mendon, N. Y., March 27, 1838, married Mary E. Shepard.

Mary E. Stoutenburg, daughter of Wm.

Note. - The Barnes Mill, Brighton, N. Y.

Before any white settlement was made in Monroe Co., N. Y., Indian Allen, a white man, built a mill at Genesee falls and ground corn for the Indians. Isaac Barnes bought the run of stones that were in Indian Allen's mill and put them in the Barnes mill at Brighton. Charles Milo Barnes donated this run of stones to the Pioneer society of Monroe Co.; and when the Monroe Co. Court house was built they were placed in the wall of the court house, on the first floor, and can be seen there to-day.

SAN FRANCISCO, CAL., AFTER THE LAST FIRE IN 1850.

In 1847 the name of the village of Yerba Buena, Cal., was changed to San Francisco, the number of inhabitants at that date being about 450. The next year gold was discovered in California, and from that time the growth of the city was rapid, and in three years the population was 25,000. In 1850 a large portion of the place was destroyed by a fire which was followed in a few days by a conflagration that almost wiped out the city. Charles Milo Barnes, who was there, sent a picture home; from which this one was engraved. See P. 147.

and Mary E. Shepard, born at Pittsford, N. Y., July 28, 1840, was married to Oscar Stoutenburg at Pittsford, N. Y., Jan. 16, 1862. They have two children, as follows:

WM. A. STOUTENBURG born at Pittsford, N. Y., Sep. 10, 1867.

CHARLOTTE E. STOUTENBURG born at Wyanet, Ill., Apr. 3, 1869.

All reside at Burt, Iowa.

Sarah Culver and Family.

SARAH F. CULVER, daughter of Wm. and Mary E. Shepard, was born at Pittsford, N. Y., May 27, 1842; is a member of the M. E. Church. She married Abram Culver, son of Cornelius Culver, at Pittsford, May 1, 1867. They moved to Michigan in 1867; are engaged in farming; P. O. address is Ypsilanti, Mich., R. F. D. No. 2; have two daughters, Nellie Barnes and Cora May.

NELLIE BARNES CULVER, born at Superior, Mich., Aug. 3, 1870, is a trained nurse. She is a member of the M. E. Church; resides at Ypsilanti, Mich.

CORA MAY CULVER, born at Superior, Mich., Feb., 22, 1872, married Emil H.

Bradford Dec. 22, 1892. They reside at 1006 Waverly Ave., Toledo, O.; are members of the Presbyterian Church; have one child, Nellie Grace, born Feb. 14, 1894.

Geo. W. and Lucy K. Farnam and Family.

GEO. W. FARNAM, son of George Washington Farnam, born Oct. 16, 1845, at Scipio, Cayuga Co., N. Y., was a soldier in the War of the Rebellion, enlisted Aug. 28, 1862, and served to the close of the war; was in the battle of Cold Harbor and the siege of Petersburg; is a farmer; married Lucy K. Shepard.

LUCY K. FARNAM, daughter of Wm. and Mary E. Shepard, born at Pittsford, N. Y., May 8, 1844, married Geo. W. Farnam. They are members of the Presbyterian Church; reside at Pittsford, N. Y.; have three children, Mary, Frank and Alfred.

MARY FARNAM married Delos Loughborough. They have four children, as follows:

TRACY LEON was born Jan. 17, 1891, at Pittsford, N. Y.

LUCY ELMA was born Apr. 29, 1893, at Batavia, N. Y.

MARIA FLORENCE was born June 8, 1896, at Batavia.

GEORGE LEROY was born Apr. 26, 1898, at Spencer, N. Y.

FRANK FARNAM was born at Pittsford, N. Y., June 12, 1870; is married and resides at Plum Point, Va.

ALFRED H. FARNAM was born at Pittsford, N. Y., Sep. 7, 1872; is married and resides at Pittsford.

WM. MILLER SHEPARD, son of Wm. and Mary Shepard, born June 2, 1846, died Nov. 19, 1889.

CHARLOTTE LOUISA SHEPARD, daughter of Wm. and Mary Shepard, born May 1, 1848, died Apr. 17, 1881.

Isaac Barnes Shepard and Family.

ISAAC BARNES SHEPARD, son of Wm. and Mary Shepard, born Dec. 1, 1852, married Jessie Heacock at Rochester, Dec. 3, 1879. They moved to Pittsford, N. Y., and resided at the old homestead; moved to Marion, Ind., in 1891; moved to Rochester, N. Y., Dec. 3, 1896, where they now reside.

He is engaged in a wood and coal business;
P. O. address is 41 Niagara St., Rochester,
N. Y. They have four children, as follows:

LOTTIE, born Sep. 13, 1881, is a stenographer and book keeper.

Katherine, born Feb. 20, 1883, is a teacher in the Public school.

ADA was born Apr. 2, 1887.

RALPH SHEPARD was born May 21, 1889.

MILON D. BARNES.

MILON D. BARNES, son of Isaac and Sarah Barnes, born at Brighton, N. Y., in 1819, died at Brighton, June 2, 1859, aged 40 years.

ANNA ELIZA (Servis) BARNES, wife of Milon D. Barnes, died Sep. 4, 1897, aged 80 years.

They had two children, Ira and Albert.

Ira Servis Barnes and Family.

IRA S. BARNES, son of Milon D. Barnes, born at Brighton, N. Y., Feb. 22, 1849, is a mason by trade; married Lucy Maria Wright at Rochester, Aug. 31, 1871. They reside at Brighton; have had three children, as follows:

ALBERT WALTER BARNES, born at Tidioute, Pa., June 2, 1872, married Caroline Jessica Barret Aug. 30, 1895, had one daughter, Anna May Barnes, born at Brighton, March 12, 1897. He died at Brighton, Aug. 20, 1898.

GEORGE MILAN BARNES, second son of Ira and Lucy Barnes, was born at Brighton, Apr. 27, 1874.

WM. CHAMPION BARNES, third son of Ira and Lucy Barnes, was born April 2, 1878.

———

ALBERT BARNES, son of Milon D. Barnes, was married, had no children, died in Colorado when about forty years old.

———

EDWIN M. BARNFS,

EDWIN MILTON BARNES, son of Isaac and Sarah Barnes, born at Brighton, N. Y., April 51, 1823, died at Brighton, N. Y., July 10, 1864, married Julia Ann Arnold.

JULIA ANN BARNES, wife of Edwin M. Barnes, born at Lee, Mass., Feb. 7, 1829, died at Brighton, N. Y., Feb. 21, 1863. Their children were Dwight F., Nellie, Maria, Edwin Arnold and Wm. S.

DWIGHT F. BARNES, born in 1854, died Sep. 5, 1855, aged one year, one month and eight days.

Nellie M. and Frank R. Palmer.

NELLIE MARIAH PALMER, daughter of Edwin M. Barnes, born at Fulton, Ill., May 25, 1857, died at Stockbridge, Mass., Dec. 8, 1892.

FRANK R. PALMER, son of Wm. H. Palmer, born at Stockbridge, Mass., May 27. 1855, married Nellie Mariah Barnes Oct. 6, 1880. They had three children as follows :

WM. PALMER, born Dec. 25, 1883.

MABEL PALMER, born June 27, 1888.

LOUISE PALMER, born May 11, 1891. All born at Stockbridge, Mass. Mr. Palmer is a farmer and resides at Stockbridege, Mass.

WM. S. BARNES, son of Edwin M. and Julia Barnes, born Nov. 24, 1862, died Jan. 24, 1863.

Edwin A. Barnes and Family.

EDWIN ARNOLD BARNES, son of Edwin M. and Julia A. Barnes, was born at Brighton, N. Y., Dec. 9, 1859; went from Brighton to Charleston, West Virginia, in July, 1882 and has been engaged there in the Wholesale Dry Goods and Notion business, ever since, being one of the firm of Abney-Barnes Co., and has been director in the Charleston National Bank for the last fifteen years. He married, Apr. 25, 1888, at Salt Sulphur Springs, West Virginia, Mabel Lander Appleton, b. at Boston, Mass., June 23, 1861. Their children are, as follows:

ARNOLD APPLETON BARNES was born at Charleston, West Va., Feb. 12, 1889.

BERNARD EDWIN BARNES was born at Charleston, West Va., May 16, 1890.

C. A. Barnes' Hunting Camp in Mich. Business and pleasure combined. *See P. 79.*
June 1, 1901.—"Shot five deer last winter, caught $150.00 worth of fur since March 1st, got a bear Monday, caught sev-
enty five trout yesterday and killed 2,000,000 mosquitos this morning."

THE CLIFF HOUSE, SAN FRANCISCO, CAL. James and Nellie Barnes and party. *See 54.*

CHAPTER VI.

JEDEDIAH BARNES,
HIS ANCESTRY, PARENTAGE AND DESCENDANTS.

JEDEDIAH BARNES b. about 1704, was perhaps grandson of Thomas Barnes, of Hartford (see p. 11); m. Abigail Warner, in Southington, Conn., Dec. 3, 1730; had two sons and two daughters, as follows:

LOIS b. June 23, 1732, ABIGAIL b. Apr. 6. 1735, JOSIAH b. Aug. 11, 1740 and SAMUEL b. Aug. 5, 1744. All were b. in Southington, Conn. (see Church Rec. P. 6).

JOSIAH BARNES had three children, Jedediah, Calvin, Lemuel and perhaps others.

Jedediah Barnes.

JEDEDIAH BARNES, son of Josiah Barnes, b. in N. Canaan, Litchfield Co., Conn.. m. Sophia Root. Their c. were Levi, Calvin, Philo and Rebecca. Calvin Barnes d. 1881; Philo m. Mr. Eaton, had one d., Roxania Hines of Ilion, N. Y. Rebecca Barnes m. Mr. Degroat. Jedediah Barnes d. near Utica, N. Y., 1840.

Levi Barnes.

LEVI BARNES, son of Jedediah Barnes, b. Feb. 25, 1796, in N. Canaan, Conn.; moved to Utica, N. Y.; was a soldier in the war of 1812; m. Susan Capron in 1818, and in 1820, with his wife and child, came from Utica, N. Y., in a sleigh, bought and moved onto a farm near Union City, Pa. He was ordained an elder in the M. E. Church in 1863; in 1834 was commissioned and served as captain of a company of militia. His wife died May 10, and he died May 19, 1877. Their children were Harriet, Charles Giles, John Vincent, Alpheus S., Levi Galusha, Susan, Nathan Sylvester, Hannah and Sophia.

HARRIET BARNES b. at Utica, N. Y., Nov. 18, 1819, m. Levi Richards. Their children were Sarah, Franklin, Emery, Lucy N., Wilber and Willard(twins), Charles A., and Elida.

SARAH, b. May, 1839, m. Wm. A. Richardson, 1859. Mr. Richardson enlisted in the Union army in 1863, served to the close of the war. They reside at Machias, N. Y.; have had six children, as follows:

ANNIE E. died young.

HATTIE A., b. 1867, m. Shirley Wilkins, c. Lizzie, b. 1887, Isme, b. 1891, Bernice, b.

1892, resides at Union City, Pa.

LUELLA, b. 1864, m. Henry Hatch, d. 1896.

ANNABEL, b. 1869, m. Elmer Drew, 1888, c. were, as follows: Ola F., b. 1890, d. 1895; Leon and Lydia, b. 1891; Myrtle, b. 1896.

L. BIRDEEN, b. 1875, m. Arthur Dills, c. Helen L., b. 1898, and Wm. Henry, b. 1900.

ALICE D., b. 1881.

GEO. F. RICHARDS, b. March 20, 1841, enlisted Aug. 30, 1862, d. in the army, 1864.

LUCY N., b. Nov. 11, 1844, m. Sept. 13, 1862, Josiah W. McIntyre, res. at Ft. Collins, Col.; c. Ola V., d., Loa Birdeen, d., Alice M., d. and Clyde b. Mar. 11, 1882.

EMERY C. RICHARDS, b. June 13, 1848, m. Irena Owen, Feb. 25, 1874, at Spring, Pa., res. at Union City, Pa.

WILBER RICHARDS, b. Feb. 20, 1852, m. Melissa McCleary; c. Evelyn, Wilber, Vera and Sybil; res. at Clarksburg, W. Va.; was mayor, P. M. and editor of Clarksburg Telegram; d. Feb. 29, 1892.

WILLARD RICHARDS, b. Feb. 20, 1852, m. Abigail Lewis; c. Lelia, res. at Conneaut, Ohio.

CHARLES A. RICHARDS, b. Feb. 3, 1855, m. Adell Woodbury; c. Frank M. and Wealthy, res. at Farnham, O.

ELIDA, b. Mar. 6, 1859, m. Andrew E. Woodbury, has three c., Anna, Verne and Jennie, res. at Conneaut, Ohio.

CHARLES GILES BARNES, b. at Union City 1822, d. Aug. 14, 1896, m. Laura Moses ; c. are Marshall, Leslie L., Adelbert, Pierrie and Pluma.

JOHN VINCENT BARNES, b. and res. at Union City, Pa., b. Aug. 7, 1825 ; m. Elizabeth Wellman ; c., as follows : Ellen A. b. Aug. 4, 1850 ; Francis L., b. Nov. 29, 1853 ; Elizabeth M., b. Sep., 1859, m. Wm. Sears, has three c., Edwin, Ellen and Velma, res. at Union City, Pa. ; Elmer E., b. Nov. 1, 1861 ; Mary, b. March 18, 1869, m. Oliver Brimer, has two c., res. at Union City, Pa.

ALPHEUS S. BARNES, b. Aug. 3, 1832, d. Feb. 19, 1893, m. Helen Parks. 1st w. and Hulda Barnes, 2nd w., c. are Fremont S., Lavilla and Harry.

LEVI GALUSHA BARNES, b. Apr. 8, 1835, m. Melissa Shelmadine, res. at Union City, Pa., has four c., as follows : Olive A. m. J. Carroll ; Alice M. m. Fletcher Carroll ; Mary S. m. J. W. Donaldson, res. at Hites,

Pa.; Emma A. m. Oscar Clark, res. at Bradford, Pa.; Jennie L., teacher in the public schools, res. at Union City, Pa.

NATHAN SYLVESTER BARNES, b. near Union City, Pa., Feb. 26, 1842, d. Dec. 19, 1878, m. Hulda Shelmadine, who was b. Aug. 13, 1847, had four c., Owen M., Minnie D., John W. and Grace J.

OWEN M. BARNES, b. Mar. 30, 1867, m. Gertie A. Nichols who was b. June 25, 1867, res. at Santa Barbara, Cal. They have had four c., as follows: Clara Delle, b. Aug. 8, 1888; Neil J. b. Aug. 19, 1890; Effie Belle, b. July 29, 1893, d. Apr. 4, 1895: Mead, b. Nov. 9, 1902.

MINNIE D., b. June 2, 1870, m. E. A. Shreve, b. Oct. 7, 1867, at Bloomfield, Pa. They have had five c., as follows: Cecile Belle, b. July 12, 1889; E. Harold, b. 1891, d. 1892; Edith Ruth, b. Jan. 29, 1893; E. Harold, b. Dec. 21, 1895, and M. Gladys, b. May 1, 1901.

JOHN W. BARNES, b. July 21, 1872; res. at Los Angeles, Cal.

GRACE J., b. Mar. 25, 1879, m. John W. Wellman who was b. Jan. 26, 1876, res. at

Union City, Pa. They have one c., Merideth L., b. June 2, 1902.

HANNAH MOORE lived near Union City, Pa., had two c., Lillie Saterlee and Cornelia Chaffee, d. 1903.

SUSAN m. Geo. Carroll ; P. O., Union City, Pa.

Calvin, Lemuel and perhaps others, sons of Josiah Barnes, had c., as follows : James Barnes ; Van Rensselaer Barnes and Samuel Barnes of Oneida Co., N. Y.; Byington Barnes of Fairport, N. Y.; Rev. Enoch Barnes of Little Falls, N. Y., P. E. in the M. E. Church, a descendant, by his mother, of Lorenzo Dow. Rev. Enoch Barnes' sister was the mother of Rev. Geo. Haddock.

George C. Haddock was a zealous anti-slavery and anti-saloon reformer. He was shot to death at the corner of Fourth and Water sts., Sioux City, Ia., on Aug. 21, 1886, by liquor dealers.

Rev. Frank C. Haddock, pastor of the M. E. Church, Lynn, Mass., author of ''The King on his Throne'', ''Hero and Martyr'', etc., is son of George C. Haddock.

PHINEAS BARNES AND DESCENDANTS.

PHINEAS BARNES, s. of Tho. Barnes(see p. 12, also note 12, p. 18),* b. July 7, 1730: com. of first Co. train band in Southington parish in Farmington, Ct., 1762, lieut., 1766, capt., 1767: rem. to Stockbridge Mass., before 1771: m. Phebe Bennet. Four of their sons were pioneer settlers of Pompey, N. Y.

WILLIAM BARNES, s. of Phineas and Phebe Barnes, b. in W. Stockbridge, Mass.; m. Sarah ———, of Gt. Barrington, Mass.: mov. to Pompey, N. Y.: had Orson and perhaps others.

ORSON BARNES, s. of Wm. and Sarah, b. at Pompey, N Y., Mar. 26, 1802: m. Eliz Phelps, of Suffield, Ct.: mov. to Onondaga Co., N. Y.: was Supt. of schools.

WM. BARNES, s. of Orson and Elizabeth, b. at Pompey, N. Y., May 28, 1824: attorney at law, founder of N. Y. State Ins. Dept.: m. Emily, d. of Thurlow and Catherine Weed, July 10, 1849: c. Thurlow and Wm.

THURLOW WEED BARNES, s. of Wm. and Emily Barnes, grad. at Harvard Col.: publisher at Boston, Mass.; m. Eda Macy Austin, of Boston, 1881.

WM. BARNES, of Albany, N. Y., s. of Wm. and Emily Barnes, grad. at Harvard Col.: journalist: m. Grace Davis, of Cincinnati, Ohio. *American Ancestry.*

EBENEZER BARNES.

EBENEZER BARNES, b. in Mass. in 1750, was perhaps s. of Ebenezer Barnes of Southington, Conn., m. Sept. 28, 1743(see p. 13).

*It is my opinion that Phineas Barnes was grandson of Thomas Barnes, Jr., of Southington, Ct. G. N. B.

He moved to Trumbull Co., O. and d. at Fowler Center in 1850, lacking only a few days of being one hundred years old ; had a son, Ebenezer.

EBENEZER BARNES, JR., a farmer, was b. and d. in Fowler, Trumbull Co., O. ; had four c., Harrison Ebenezer, Wm., Carmi and Ruth.

HARRISON E. BARNES, moved to Gould. O., where he d., had two sons, Albert and Newel A.

NOTE.— Chapter VI concludes the notes and records of all of the descendants of Thomas Barnes of Hartford that we have been able to obtain: but, evidently, they include the smaller part of this branch of the Barnes people. Timothy, Josiah, Phineas and Ebenezer Barnes were but four of many great grandsons of Thomas Barnes of Hartford who were heads of families when the Revolutionary War commenced: and many Barnes people who have no knowledge of their forefathers, were it possible, could trace their ancestry back to Thomas Barnes who was, perhaps, the first Barnes to come to America, and the ancestor of the largest branch of the family in the United States.

CHAPTER VII.

THOMAS BARNES OF NEW HAVEN.

MOSES BARNES, ELISHA BARNES AND OTHERS.

THOMAS BARNES of New Haven, son of Thomas Barnes of England, born about 1623, died at Middleton, Ct., 1693.
Children.—John, Thomas, Daniel, Maybee and Elizabeth.—See p. 7.

MAYBEE BARNES, son of Thomas Barnes of New Haven, born June 25, 1663, died March 6, 1748, m. Elizabeth Stowe, 1693.
Children.—Nathaniel and perhaps Daniel.

DANIEL BARNES, perhaps son of Maybee Barnes, born April, 1701, died May 24, 1775. He was a deacon in the church and captain of train band ; m. Zuriah Edgar, daughter of Abraham and Lydia Edgar.
Children.—Moses and perhaps Elijah and Elisha.

MOSES BARNES, son of Daniel Barnes, born Dec., 1740, m. Sarah Banister, had a son,

Abijah, enlisted in the Continental Army, Feb. 1, 1777, served one year, reenlisted, was promoted to captain and was discharged in 1783.

ABIJAH BARNES, son of Moses Barnes, born in Litchfield, Conn., Jan. 3, 1770, died in Mass., May 20, 1833. His family consisted of nine children, as follows: Anna, Daniel, Stephen, Hosea, Abigail, Hulda, Abijah, Norman and Robert; *wife: Abi Brayford, b. Jan. 3, 17?*

Wales.

ANNA HARMON, daughter of Abijah Barnes born in Erie Co., Pa., Apr. 6, 1789, m. Mr. Harmon, had four children, Appleton, Sophronia, Amos and Ansil, d. Jan. 14, 1847.

APPLETON HARMON, born May 29, 1820, died at Holden, Utah, Feb. 27, 1877.

SOPHRONIA HARMON, born April 5, 1824, died at Florence, Neb.. Jan. 27, 1847.

AMOS HARMON, born Oct. 30, 1827, resides at Messina, Cal.

ANSIL HARMON, born in Erie Co., Pa., Apr. 5, 1832, resides at Holden, Utah.

DANIEL BARNES, son of Abijah Barnes, born in Mass., March 11, 1799, moved to Erie Co, Pa, where he died May 16, 1867, married Philinda Martin.

PHILINDIA M. Barnes, wife of Daniel Barnes, born September 22, 1808, died June 14, 1848. Their family consisted of seven children, as follows:

ALFRED BARNES, born July 13, 1832, died June 29, 1848.

MARY ANN BARNES, born Feb. 12, 1833, died in Wilson, Kansas, Mar. 26, 1870.

BETSY BARNES, born May 4, 1837, died Aug. 12, 1842.

ABIGAIL BARNES, born Nov. 7, 1839, P. O. is Mansfield, O.

NANCY BARNES, born Apr. 1, 1841, P. O. address is Albion, Pa.

CLARINDA BARNES, born Oct. 19, 1842, died at Omaha, Neb., Feb. 2, 1902.

DANIEL BARNES, Jr., born June 2, 1848, in Erie Co., Pa., went to Kansas in 1869, m. Louesa Pugh Dec. 8, 1880. They have two daughters, Mina born Oct. 5, 1882, and Ruby born April 6, 1894. They reside at Cedar Vale, Kansas.

STEPHEN BARNES, son of Abijah Barnes, born in Mass., Oct. 8, 1800, moved with his parents to Conneaut Tp., Erie Co., Pa., in 1818: was 1st Lt. of a company of state militia : received his commission April 18, 1828. He married Margaret Walker Apr. 20, 1826 ; moved to La Salle Co., Ill., in 1844, where he died July 17, 1853.

Margaret W. Barnes, wife of Stephen Barnes, born in Crawford Co., Pa., May 2, 1806, died at State Centre, Io, May 7, 1867. Their children were Rebecca H., William. Sarah Jane and Abi.

Rebecca H., born in Erie Co., Pa., Nov. 27, 1827, m. Mr. R. R. Bullock Nov. 19, 1848, has three sons, Franklin, Henry and William E. P. O. address, State Centre, Io.

I daughter Lilly m.   m. Walter Fay.

William Barnes, born March 24, 1830, died Jan. 10, 1901, at Chicago, Ill., and was buried at Hillside, one mile north of State Centre, Iowa. He married Jennett L. Mead.

Jennett L. Barnes, lives near Charlotte, Mich., R. F. D., No. 1 ; was married to William Barnes in Erie Co., Pa., Dec. 24, 1854, had two sons, Stephen Jay and Robert Lisle.

Stephen Jay Barnes, born June 22, 1857, married Isabel Cleland Feb. 22, 1882, has two children, Le Roy Wm., born July 27, 1888, and Mabel Margaret, born April 18,

1890, lives at White Lake, South Dakota.

ROBERT LISLE BARNES, born in Marshall Co., Iowa, April 23, 1866, married Elberta Taylor Dec. 3, 1885, has one child, Florence M. Barnes, born Dec. 19, 1889, resides at 375 Bissell St., Chicago, Ill.

SARAH JANE, born Feb. 1, 1834, married Albert G. Bullock Aug. 22, 1853, has two daughters, Ida M. Grooms and Ella Welton. They reside at Saratoga, Wyoming.

ABI, born in Erie Co., Pa., May 15, 1837, married Abraham N. Woolston March 24, 1859. They reside at State Centre, Iowa; have six children, as follows:
DELLA MARGARET BOND, Lathrop, Cal.
LEONARD L. WOOLSTON, Lathrop, Cal.
HOMER WM. WOOLSTON, Cheyenne, Wyo.
MAY E. SMITH, Marshalltown, Io.
ETHEL L. WOOLSTON. State Centre, Io.
STANLEY BARNS WOOLSTON, State Centre, Io.

HOSEA BARNES, s. of Abijah Barnes, born at New Ashford, Berkshire Co., Mass., Jan. 9, 1802, m. Betsey Marcy, died July 9, 1891, in Conneaut Tp., Erie Co., Pa.

BETSEY M. BARNES, born Aug. 6, 1815,

m. Hosea Barnes July 3, 1839, died April 4, 1895. They had three children, Lydia, Robert Adolphus and Ira Henry.

LYDIA, born May 22, 1840, m. Henry Brown. Their children are Norah, Katie, Frederick and Bonnie B. P. O. Albion, Pa.

ROBERT A. BARNES, b. Dec. 12, 1842, in Conneaut Tp., Erie Co., Pa., has been engaged continuously in mercantile business in Albion, Pa., since 1866, m. Lucy Harrington.

LUCY H. BARNES, born Feb. 15, 1842, m. Robert A. Barnes Sep. 5, 1866. They have four children, as follows : Harley J., Hattie M., Cassius M. and Bessie.

HARLEY J. BARNES, born Nov. 24, 1870, is a member of the firm of R. A. Barnes & Son, dealers in Dry Goods, Groceries &c. m. Katie Howard Dec. 24, 1891, has one son, Robert Howard Barnes, born May 24, 1893, resides at Albion, Erie Co., Pa.

HATTIE M., born Aug. 30, 1873, m. Emory F. Bristol, Sep. 29, 1898, lives at Albion, Pa.

CASSIUS M. BARNES, born at Albion, Pa., Sep. 18, 1876, a graduate of Philadelphia

Dental College, m. Nellie Spaulding.

NELLIE BARNES, born Sep. 26, 1877, married Cassius M. Barnes June 28, 1900. They live at Albion, Pa.

BESSIE BARNES was born Jan. 18, 1885.

ABIGAIL, daughter of Abijah Barnes, born March 27, 1804, m. Mr. Bacon, died 1837.

HULDAH BARNES, daughter of Abijah Barnes, born Oct. 1, 1806, died Sept. 20, 1898, was a strong, vigorous woman, both in mind and body, retaining her faculties unimpaired until after ninety years of age. She traveled much, taking notes along the way, and left quite a volume of notes and records of her father's family and ancestors, which, through the courtesy of Ansil Harmon, the author has had the benefit of in compiling this work.

ABIJAH BARNES, son of Abijah Barnes, born in Mass. Apr. 14, 1808, m. Mary Blackwell, had five children, George, Hiram Abijah, Harriet, Eliza and Matilda, died in Conneaut Tp., Erie Co., Pa., Jan. 26, 1875.

GEORGE BARNES son of Abijah Barnes born

in Erie Co., Pa., June 4, 1835, died March 4, 1902, m. Lizzie Ann Sherman, who was born in Cattaraugus Co., N. Y., Feb. 21, 1845, had one daughter, Lulia Louisa, born Oct. 17, 1865, m. Clinton Thompson, P. O., Conneaut, O.

HIRAM A. BARNES, son of Abijah and Mary Barnes, born March 4, 1845, m. Louisa Hannah, had three children, Hiram and two died young.

HIRAM BARNES, son of Hiram A. Barnes, born 1876, m. Ella Dewey, has one son, Glenn.

HARRIET, daughter of Abijah and Mary Barnes, born 1837, m. Edmund C. Smith in 1856, had two children, P. O., R. F. D., No. 2, Erie, Pa.

WILLIS H. SMITH, son of Edmund and Harriet Smith born in 1858 m. to Nellie Reed in 1887 lives at W. Springfield, Pa.

ELIZA, daughter of Abijah and Mary Barnes, born in 1840, m. Willard Martindale. They have had seven children, three born in Pa. are dead; four born in Kansas, Leroy, Mary, Nora and Harriet, reside at Moline, Elk Co., Kansas.

MATILDA, born Feb. 17, 1843, m. Walter Kirtland.

NORMAN BARNES, son of Abijah Barnes, born Nov. 16, 1810, m. Sarah Ann Marcy, had eleven children, seven died in infancy, Frank and Mrs. Ed Orton live at Kenosha. Wis., the other two are dead. .

ROBERT BARNES, son of Abijah Barnes, born at New Ashford, Berkshire Co., Mass., Feb. 23, 1813, died Apr. 6, 1903. His wife, Mary Ann Barnes, was born at Hamburg, Erie Co., N. Y., Aug. 14, 1818, died June 11, 1865. They had five children, all born at Pleasant Prairie, Wis., as follows :

WARREN, born Oct. 22, 1835, died Nov. 8, 1842.

HOSEA, born Dec. 18, 1837, resides at Kenosha, Wis.

LOUISA B. MCDONALD, born Dec. 15, 1839, resides at Limestone, N. Y.

MARY A. MEEKER, born Jan 27, 1858, resises at Lily Dale, N. Y.

JOHN BARNES, born July 20, 1846, died Jan. 19, 1850.

ELISHA BARNES.

ELISHA BARNES,* born about 1752, was a soldier in the Revolutionary War. He enlisted May 24, 1776, was promoted to corporal.—His. Reg. Con. Army.

Elisha Barnes, Jr., and Family.

ELISHA BARNES, JR., son of Elisha Barnes, born in New York in 1795, moved to Trumbull Co., Ohio, died in 1848. His brothers and sisters were Elijah, William, Moses, Clara Perkins and Betsey Silliman. His children were Francis, Wm. Lemuel, Orlan Henry, Olive, Mariah and Mary.

FRANCIS BARNES, son of Elisha Barnes, Jr., had five children, Francis, John, Emily, and Mahalah. Francis died young.

ISAAC BARNES lives at the old homestead in Beaver Tp., Crawford Co., Pa.

JOHN BARNES lives at Willoughby, O.: has had seven children, Amy, Laura, Ella, Jessie and two whose names are not given. Two are dead.

---

* Elisha Barnes was probably son of Daniel Barnes (See P. 173). People who were reliable have told me that Daniel Barnes had four sons, Moses, Elisha, Elijah and Timothy, and one thought that he also had another son William.

John Barnes m. Stella Southward June 22, 1890. Amy E. was b. Apr. 13, 1891. Eleanor May was b. Apr. 28, 1894. Laura N. was b. Oct. 12, 1895, d. Nov. 6, 1902. Jessie E. was b. Apr. 25, 1897. David Allen was b. March 8, 1901. Ruth Bernice was b. May 10, 1903.

EMILY M. IRISH, daughter of Francis Barnes, b. Dec. 4, 1847, m. James Barton Sep. 10, 1866. They had five children, as follows : Francis, Larell, Walter, Robert, and Freddie. Mr. Barton, husband of Emily Barton, died June 1, 1896. She married Albert G. Irish April 1, 1900, P. O. Conneautville, Pa.

FRANCIS BARTON, born Apr. 6, 1870, m. Ora Holcomb Dec. 31, 1889, has two children, Lucius b. July 30, 1891, and Ona b. Aug. 30, 1894. His P. O. is Conneautville, Pa.

LARELL BARTON was born May 17, 1874.

WALTER BARTON, b. July 6, 1876, m. May Bell Holcomb, has one son, Owen. P. O. is Conneaut, Ohio.

ROBERT BARTON was born March 20, 1884.

FREDDIE BARTON was born July 13, 1883.

MAHALIA IRISH, daughter of Francis Barnes, b. Feb. 25, 1852, m. Henry Irish Jan. 1, 1871, had one daughter, Hattie.

HATTIE IRISH, b. Sep. 5, 1875, m. Wm. Parker Aug. 5, 1893, has one daughter, Hazel. b. June 9, 1894. P. O. address is Conneautville, Pa.

Wm. L. Barnes and Family.

WM. L. BARNES, second son of Elisha Barnes, Jr., was born in Trumbull Co., O., May 23, 1824; served one year in the War of the Rebellion in Co. G., 1st Wis. Cav.; died in Pierpont, Ohio, in 1902; was married to Julia Mapes. They had eight children, as follows: Wilson E., Francis A., Amy R., Mary M., Cordelia A., Stephen Elisha, Wm. Allen and Maggie Almira.

WILSON E. BARNES was born in Beaver, Crawford Co., Pa., June 18, 1855; married Mary Flickinger of Columbiana Co., O.; has one son, Roscoe, born March 2, 1891.

FRANCIS A. BARNES, born in Beaver, Crawford Co., Pa., Oct. 30, 1856, m. Sarah Wilson, has five children, as follows: Rolla, born in July, 1877; Frank; Clara, born March 12, 1883, m. David Burket; John, born Aug. 21, 1890, and Clifford, born Aug. 23, 1899.

AMY ROSETTA, born Sep. 20, 1853, m. Allen Cadwalader, has one daughter, Elma, born Aug. 6, 1888.

MARY M., born near Conneautville, Pa., March 26, 1861, m. Frank Cole, has two daughters, Rosa, born Jan. 15, 1887, and Ella, born Jan. 10, 1890.

CORDELIA AUGUSTA, born at Fort Howard, Wis., Sep. 12, 1866, m. Wm. Campbell. They have four children, Mamie, born July 7, 1883; Leroy, born Oct. 26, 1887; Glenn, born Aug. 3, 1890, and Howard, born Jan., 1898.

STEPHEN ELISHA BARNES was born in Ashtabula Co., O., March 26, 1870. He married Martha Keyes. They have four children, Emery Alfred, born June 4, 1890; Florence A., born Nov., 1893; Nellie, born Sep., 1896, and Elmo, born April, 1899.

WILLIAM A. BARNES, born at Howland,

Trumbull Co., O., June 16, 1875, m. Lelia
Irene Squires Oct. 17, 1894. They live at
Pierpont, Ohio; have four children, as fol-
lows: Walter Allen, born May 9, 1896;
Hermon Winfred, born Oct. 18, 1898;
Evylene, born April 18, 1901, and baby
born in 1903.

MAGGIE ALMIRA, born Sep. 3, 1878, m.
Earnest Trisket Jan. 1, 1898. They live at
Perry, O.; have three sons, Clarence Hen-
ry, born Dec. 18, 1898; Elmer Frank, born
July 28, 1900, and baby born in 1902.

ORLAN HENRY BARNES, third son of Eli-
sha Barnes, Jr., born Aug. 3, 1836, m.
Cyntha Jacket. Their children were Ada
Jane, Eva L., Ella E. and Frankie J.

ADA JANE, born July 4, 1860, m. Frank
Knapp, has one son, Lynn O. Knapp, m.
in 1903, A. H. Stager, lives at Conneaut, O.

EVA L., born July 3, 1863, m. Edmond L.
Gordon. They live at Ashtabula, O.; have
had four children, as follows: Edmond R.,
born March 3, 1882; Jessie E.; Don G.,
and Dorothy.

ELLA E., born Jan. 21, 1866, m. 1st, Wood

Caldwell, had two children, Cora E. and Hazel. m. 2nd, Hugh Sutherland, had one child, Vasser. They live at Ashtabula, O.

FRANKIE died young.

OLIVE, daughter of Elisha Barnes, Jr., born Apr. 27, 1832, m. 1st, Austin Calhoun, had one daughter, Lois ; m. 2nd, Richard Waterman. They lived near Beaver Centre, Pa.

LOIS, daughter of Austin and Olive Calhoun, born Oct. 3, 1850, m. Edgar Saeger, of Saegerstown, Pa., has one daughter, Ollie, who m. Mead Lawrence of Beaver Centre, Pa.

MARIA, second daughter of Elisha Barnes, Jr., born in 1839, m. Eli Broughton. Their children were Sophrona, Mary, Eunice, Sarah, Elisha, Eli, Orlan and Edith. All live in Minn.

MARY, third daughter of Elisha Barnes, Jr., born March 6, 1841, m. Joseph Dewolf. Thy had two children, Harra and Mabel. Harra m. Carrie Sterns, had one daughter, Emma. Mabel m. Silas Law, had four children, Bertha, Bessie, Walter, and Mabel.

CHAPTER VIII.

GENEALOGICAL RECORDS.

JOSHUA BARNES OF YARMOUTH, TIMOTHY BARNES
OF CONN., AND OTHERS.

DESCENDANTS OF JOSHUA BARNES
OF YARMOUTH.

1 SAMUEL BARNES.

Samuel Barnes of Easthampton, L. I., s. of Joshua
Barnes of Yarmouth, b. 1649. *See p. 4.*

2 STEPHEN BARNES.

Stephen Barnes of Bradford, Ct., probably s. of Samuel Barnes of Easthampton, b. at Southampton, L. I.,
m. Mary Barnes, moved there about 1700, died at Bradford; had a son, Stephen.

3 STEPHEN BARNES.

Stephen Barnes, s. of Stephen Barnes of Bradford, b.
Jan. 2, 1704, m. Martha Wheadon; removed to Southington, Ct., located in S. W. part of town, d. March 27, 1777.

Children—Mary, Stephen, Jonathan, William, Nathan,
Asa.

12 STEPHEN BARNES.

Stephen Barnes, s. of Stephen (3), b. Dec. 3, 1728, m.
1751, Sarah Barnes, d. Aug. 26, 1784.

Children—Sarah; Philemon, b. June 26, 1757; Farring-
ton, b. Dec. 2, 1760, m. Sally Talmage, moved to North-
ampton, Mass.; Mark, b. March 12, 1764, m. Sarah Roberts; Martha; Nathan, b. Jan. 8, 1771, m. Elizabeth ——.

13 JONATHAN BARNES.

Jonathan Barnes, s of Stephen Barnes (3), b. Feb. 2,
1731, m. Aug. 4, 1757, Elizabeth Woodruff. He died
Jan. 7, 1807.

Children—Jonathan, Elizabeth, Mary, Stephen, Sylvia,
Lois, Levi, Joel, Truman.

15 WILLIAM BARNES.

William Barnes, s. of Stephen Barnes (3), b. Nov. 10,
1738, m. Martha Upson; was captain; removed to North-
ampton, Mass., 1800.

Children—Hannah, Azuba; Benjamin, b. October 6,
1761; Experience; William, b. Feb. 2, 1767; Elizabeth.

17 ASA BARNES.

Asa Barnes, s. of Stephen Barnes (3), b. Aug. 24, 1745,
m. Oct. 30, 1765, Phebe Atkins. He lived in S. W. part
of Southington, Ct., kept tavern, gave a ball in honor of
French officers.

Children—Allen, b. July 16, 1767; Naomi, Selah, Ruth;
Martin, died young; Eli, b. May 21, 1775; Asa, b. July
22, 1777; Martin, died young; Ira, b. Nov. 15, 1781; Philo,
b. March 2, 1782.

19 PHILEMON BARNES.

Philemon, s. of Stephen Barnes (12) b. June 26, 1757,
m. June 10, 1779, Anna Scott, in Wolcott, Ct., died there
Jan. 29, 1795.

Children—Fanny, Mary; Stephen, b. May 9, 1784;
Laura; Cyrenius, b. March 15, 1790.

24 JONATHAN BARNES.

Jonathan Barnes, s. of Jonathan Barnes (13), b. March

13, 1763, m. Feb. 19, 1789, Rachel Steel. He graduated at Yale College in 1784, studied law, was State's attorney for Tolland Co.; died Sept. 24, 1829.

Children—Jonathan, b. Nov. 21, 1789; Julius S., b. Feb. 23, 1792; Eliza; William, b. Feb. 8, 1802; Mariah; Josiah, b. May 26, 1804; graduated at Yale College and at Med. Univ. of Pa.; d. 1871.

27 STEPHEN BARNES.

Stephen Barnes, s. of Jonathan Barnes (13) b. Feb. 12, 1769, m. Sally Andrews, Nov. 14, 1823; was captain of cavalry.

Children—Eunice, Alva Saxton, Polla M., Leonard Merriman; Edwin, b. May 29, 1799; Truman, b. 1801, d. 1829; Liva, 1804; Stephen A., Aug. 28, 1809, d. 1854.

31 JOEL BARNES.

Joel Barnes, s. of Jonathan Barnes (13) b. 1779, m. Rebecca Stevens, d. March 15, 1819.

Children—Caroline, Norman S., Matilda, Eunice; Joel H., b. June 7, 1813; Reuben, b. Dec. 9, 1315.

32 TRUMAN BARNES.

Truman Barnes, s. of Jonathan Barnes (13), b. April 23, 1783; m. Jan. 3, 1805, Lowly Barrett.
Children—Mary, Lowly, Emily, Sylvia.

40 ALLEN BARNES.

Allen Barnes, s. of Asa Barnes (17) b. July 16, 1767, m. Sarah Webster, d. Sept. 27, 1809.

41 SELAH BARNES.

Selah Barnes, s. of Asa Barnes (17) b. March 4, 1769, m. Oct. 9, 1791, Nancy Cowls, who died April 7, 1831; m. Dec. 28, 1831, Ada Clark. He died Oct. 15, 1850; had 13 children.

Children—Charles C., b. Feb. 8, 1792, d. in 1813; Elihu, died young; Phebe, Laura; Martha, b. Jan. 8,

1801, m. Rev. Charles Goodrich, missionary to Sandwich Islands; William, b. April 11, 1803, d. June 11, 1852; Amzi, b. Aug. 5, 1805; Nancy, Selah; Charles, b. Oct. 30, 1813; Allen, b. June 23, 1816; Henry E., b. Oct. 31, 1832.

44 ELI BARNES.

Eli Barnes, s. of Asa Barnes (17), b. May 21, 1775, in Southington, Ct., d. at Barnesville 1829. He was a farmer, was engaged in real estate business, founded the village of Barnesville, now a part of New Haven, Ct.; m. Nov. 4, 1795, Roxana Newell; m. (2) Aug. 2, 1812, Susan M. Bradley.

Children—Jeremiah R., b. March 9, 1809; Alfred Smith, b. Jan. 28, 1817; John C., b. 1828.

45 ASA BARNES.

Asa Barnes, s. of Asa Barnes (17), b. July 22, 1777, m. Polly Woodruff; lived in Southington, Ct., d. July 6, 1806.

Children—Henry, b. July 13, 1806; Benjamin, b. July 13, 1806; Reuben, b. April 14, 1811; Edmond, b. May 2, 1813; Dennis, b. 1818.

47 PHILO BARNES.

Philo Barnes, s. of Asa Barnes, (17), b. March 2, 1782, m. Amanda Pond, July 4, 1802; m.(2) Electa Durin; lived in Marion district, Southington, Ct.

Children—Martin, Seth, Emily; Harriet, b. Oct. 29, 1806, m. Henry Beecher; Rhoda; Rollin R., b. Jan. 17, 1811, drowned Sept., 1828; Sylvia; Martin, b. Mary 31, 1819; Willard Ira, b. Dec. 25, 1820; Jennette; Seth E., b. Nov. 13, 1824, d. July 20, 1863, from wounds received at Ft. Wagner; Andrew F., b. Aug. 16, 1827.

55 JONATHAN BARNES.

Jonathan Barnes, s. of Jonathan Barnes (24), b. in Tolland Nov. 21, 1789, m. April 29, 1819, Maria Ward.

He graduated at Yale College, 1830, was a lawyer, lived at Middleton; d. Dec. 24, 1861.

Children—Jane Jones, Catherine Rogers; Jonathan E., b. Feb. 8, 1828; Henry W., b. Feb. 10, 1830.

56 JULIUS S. BARNES.

Julius S. Barnes, s. of Jonathan Barnes (24), b. in Tolland Feb. 23, 1792, m. Laura Lewis; graduated at Yale College in 1815, was M. D., lived at Southington, Ct.; d. Nov. 12, 1870.

Children—Randolf, b. April 7, 1823, d. Nov. 1, 1849; Lewis, graduated at Yale College; is M. D., lives at Oxford, Ct.; Julius, b. Aug. 25, 1831; John J., b. April 14, 1834.

64 EDWIN BARNES.

Edwin Barnes, s. of Stephen Barnes (27), b. May 29, 1799, m. (1) Lucy Smith; (2) Frances M. Bristol; lives at Southington, Ct.

Children—Henry S., b. Nov. 21, 1823; Edwin D., b. March 26, 1838; Julius B., b. Oct. 10, 1840.

66 LIVA BARNES.

Liva Barnes, s. of Stephen Barnes (27) b. July 5, 1809, m. Lucretia C. DeWoolf, d. Nov. 12, 1872; lived in Southington, Ct.

Children—Truman, b. March 8, 1835; Liva F., b. July 1, 1837.

92 HENRY E. BARNES.

Rev. Henry E. Barnes, s. of Selah Barnes (41), b. Oct. 31, 1832, m. Eliza Carpenter May 1, 1862.

Children—Harra E., b. Jan. 24, 1863; Ralf N. C., b. Sept. 4, 1870; Roy T. H., b. Dec. 28, 1871.

93 JEREMIAH R. BARNES.

Rev. Jeremiah R. Barnes, s. of Eli Barnes (44), b. March 9, 1809, m. (1) Catherine Platt Aug. 7, 1836; m. (2)

Catherine Webster; graduated at Yale College 1834, taught academy at Southington, pastor of Presbyterian church at Evansville, Ind., 9 years, at Piqua, O., 2 years; in 1850 pub. the Western Emporium at Cincinnati, O.; was agent of Miss. association.

Children Charles J.,b. July 26, 1837; Julia A., b. Aug. 27, 1840, m. July 2, 1867, Prof. Geo. R. Gear, of Marietta College; Catherine P., b. July 16, 1844; Caroline W., b. July 14, 1846.

97 ALFRED S. BARNES.

Alfred Smith Barnes, s. of Eli Barnes (44), b. at Barnesville, Ct., Jan. 28, 1817, d. at Brooklyn, N. Y., Feb. 17, 1888. He was a philantropist; was Sr. member of the publishing firm of A. S. Barnes & Co., N. Y., and Brooklyn, N. Y.; married Nov. 21, 1841, Harriet Elizabeth, daughter of Brig. Gen. Timothy Burr, who served in war of 1812.

Children—Alfred C., b. Oct. 27, 1842; Mary C., b. May 25, 1844, m. Rev. Charles Ray Palmer of Bridgeport, Ct., Henry Burr, b. Dec. 14, 1845.

100 JOHN C. BARNES.

John C. Barnes, s. of Eli Barnes (44), b. Aug. 15, 1823, m. Mary Starr; in business in N. Y.

Children—Charles W., b. Oct. 20, 1851; Thomas R., b. Jan. 15, 1857; Alfred S., b. Jan. 12, 1858.

185 CHARLES J. BARNES.

Charles J. Barnes, s. of Jeremiah R. Barnes (93), b. July 26, 1837, at Evansville, Ind., m. Mary Ludington of Chicago, Ill., March 27, 1868. He is connected with the firm of A. S. Barnes & Co., publishers, Chicago, ,N. Y. and Cinn.; resides at Chicago.

189 ALFRED BARNES.

Alfred C. Barnes, s. of Alfred Smith Barnes (97) b.

Oct. 27, 1842, m. Josephine E. Richardson of Brooklyn, N. Y.

Children—Harriet J., b. Aug. 7, 1864; Mary G., b. Sept. 23, 1867; Alfred V., b. July 25, 1870.

193 HENRY BURR BARNES.

Henry Burr Barnes, s. of Alfred Smith Barnes (97), b. N. Y. city Dec. 24, 1845; graduate of Yale College 1866, M. A.; editor of International Review 1877-80; publisher, house of A. S. Barnes & Co.; president of Stationers' Bd. of Trade 1887-8; m. June 16, 1869, Hannah Elizabeth, daughter of Courtland Palmer Dixon.—*See Savage's Gen Dic.; American Ancestry; Rev. Herman R. Timlow's Eccl. sketches of Southington, Ct.*

SHAMGER BARNES.

HIS ANCESTORS AND DESCENDANTS.

---

1 SHAMGER BARNES.

It is stated that Shamger Barns was the son of Charles Barns, who was born in Mass., (Lynn, perhaps) about 1640, and that Charles Barns was the son of Joshua (*See p. 4*) or of William Barns, born in East Winch, Norfolk Co., England, about 1620.

Shamger Barns, b. in E. Hampton, Long Island, in 1670; d. in E. Middleton, Ct., Dec. 13, 1750; m. Elizabeth Stead, dau. of John Stead.

Children—Mary Barns, b. 1697; John, b. 1699; Abigail and Phoebe; all born in E. Middletown, Ct., and baptized Apr. 11, 1708.

2 MARY BARNS.

Mary Barnes, dau. of Shamger Barns (1), b. about 1697, d. Sept. 17, 1734; m. Samuel Bidwell, Jr., of Middletown, Ct., Sept. 2, 1714, d. March, 1727.

Children—Daniel, b. Nov. 18, 1716; Sarah, b. Jan. 29, 1719.

3 JOHN BARNS.

John Barnes, s. of Shamger Barnes (1), b. in E. Middletown, Ct., 1699, died in E. Middletown, Ct., buried Sept. 8, 1783; m. Eunice Tryon Aug. 18, 1726. She was dau. of Abel Tryon; born Feb. 10, 1706, buried April 10, 1786.

Children—John, b. in E. Middletown, Ct., Nov. 22, 1726, d. Jan. 21, 1798; Elizabeth, b. Apr. 23, 1728; Eunice, b. July 23, 1730; Charles, b. Sept. 12, 1732; Abiah, b. July 2, 1742, d. March 6, 1762; Abel, b. Aug. 18, 1744; Jabez.

12 JABEZ BARNS.

Jabez Barns, s. of John Barns (3), lost at sea or d. of fever in the W. Indies about 1780; m. Martha Atkins March 22, 1758. She was dau. of Thomas Atkins and Martha Miller; b. in Middletown, Ct., June 17, 1739, d. Oct. 10, 1834.

Children—Daniel, b. Aug. 26, 1760; Abiah, b. Aug. 9, 1762, d. Jan. 31, 1765; Abiah, b. Apr. 27, 1765; Jabez, b. Dec. 18, 1767; Martha, b. Apr. 26, 1770; Elisha, b. July 24, 1773; Ithamar, b. Apr. 12, 1776, d. May 7, 1849; Levi, b. May, 1778; Elizur, b. Sept. 20, 1780.

13 DANIEL BARNS.

Daniel Barns, s. of Jabez Barns (12), b. Aug. 26, 1760, d. Oct. 20, 1824; married and moved probably to Steuben, Oneida Co. His wife, Sarah, b. Jan. 17, 1768, d. Oct. 5, 1833.

Children—Harriet, born Dec. 12, 1790; Olive, b. July 12, 1792, d. March 24, 1826; Sarah, b. Sept. 25, 1795; Halsey,

b. Oct. 12, 1797; Ethelbert, b. June 15, 1802; Elizur, b. May 15, 1804.

17 ELISHA BARNS.

Elisha Barns, s. of Jabez Barns (12), b. in Middletown, Ct., July 24, 1773, d. in Long Hill, East District, Ct., June 9, 1841; m. Mary Plumb Sept. 26, 1802 She was dau. of Reuben Plumb and Mary Shepherd, of Middletown, Ct.; b. Jan 2. 1775; died Feb. 19, 1809.

Children—Betsey, b. July 14. 1803, d. 1868; Mary Ann, b. June 18, 1805, d. in Attica, N. Y., Oct. 10, 1849; Emily, b. May 5, 1807, d. in Kent, Portage Co., O , Jan. 15, 1877; Caroline, b 1809, d. in Attica, N. Y., 1836; m. Parmenio Adams.

Elisha Barns (17), m. a second wife, Lucy Jones. She d. in Middletown, Ct., Nov. 24, 1854, aged about 80 years.

Children—Asher Fairchild, b. June 17, 1810, d. in Clarksburg, W. Va., Oct. 28, 1890; Duane, b. in Long Hill District, Middletown, Ct.. Feb. 18, 1814, d. in Middletown Sept. 22, 1900.

18 ITHAMAR BARNES.

Ithamar Barnes, s. of Jabez Barns (12), b. Apr. 12, 1776, d. May 7, 1849; moved to the western part of Ct., Roxbury, perhaps; m. Amy Thomas. She was b. Jan. 3, 1783, d. June 19, 1853.

Children—Elizur, b. Oct. 19, 1801; Hiram, b. Oct. 27, 1802; Samantha, b. Sept. 3, 1804; Polly, b. March 22, 1807; Nelson, b. Dec. 18, 1808; Charles, b. Oct 21, 1810, d. June 5, 1887; Asahel T., b. June 6, 1813; Horace, b. Apr. 28, 1817, d. Oct. 3, 1338; George, b Jan. 4, 1819; Sherwood, b. Nov. 6, 1821, d. Sept. 28. 1873; Richard, b. Oct. 13, 1823; Phebe A., b. Apr. 7, 1825.

20 ELIZUR BARNES.

Elizur Barnes, s. of Jabez Barnes (12), b. in Middletown, Ct., Sept. 20, 1870, d. in Middletown, Ct., Feb.,

1825, m. Clarissa Bacon Dec. 1, 1804. She was b. about 1782, d. Jan. 11, 1869

Children—Richard Edward b. 1805, d. 1822: Mary Martha b. in Middletown, Ct., Jan.25, 1808, d. Apr. 28, 1869: Frederic b. in Middletown, Ct., Feb. 27, 1810, was a sea captain, d. of cholera at New Orleans, La., in 1849: Clarissa b. March 3, 1812; Amelia b. Feb. 19, 1814, d. 1872: Elizur b. in Middletown Ct., March 29, 1817: Lucius b. Aug. 1, 1819, d. 1836: Lucy Garfield b. June 9, 1823, d. March 7, 1875: Richard Edward b. in Middletown, Ct., June 9, 1823, d. May 9, 1899.

28 MARY ANN BARNES GOULD.

Mary Ann Barnes, dau. of Elisha Barnes (17), b. in Long Hill, Ct., June 18, 1805, d. in Attica, N. Y., Oct. 10, 1849, m. in Genesee Co., N. Y., Ozro Amander Gould May 1, 1832. He was b. in Rutland, Vt., 1808, d. in Toronto, Canada, Dec. 15, 1845.

Children—Ozro Barnes Gould b. in Oxford, Canada, Apr. 17, 1840.

29 EMILY BARNES DE FOREST.

Emily Barnes, dau. of Elisha Barnes (17), b. in Long Hill, Middletown, Ct., May 15, 1807, d. in Kent, Portage Co., O., Jan. 15, 1877, m. Curtis De Forest Aug. 1827. He was b. at Barkhamstead, Ct., July 12, 1857: d. at Kent, O., Jan. 11, 1881.

Children—Elisha b. 1828, d. 1829: Caroline b. Feb. 1, 1830, d. at Newton Falls, O., March 1890 or 93: Ladoiskie b. 1833, d, 1837; William b. at Attica, N. Y., Mar. 2, 1837, d. at Kent, O., March 9, 1853: Derwin b. 1838: Murry, d. young: Charles b. June 11, 1846, d. March 20, 1865.

31 ASHER FAIRCHILD BARNES.

Asher Fairchild Barnes, son of Elisha Barnes (17), b. at Long Hill, Ct., June 17, 1801, d. in Clarksburg, W. Va., Oct. 28, 1890. He m. Adeline Scovill in Saybrook, Ashtabula Co., O., Feb. 2, 1831. She was b. in Saybrook, Ct., August 2, 1 12, d. in Clarksburg, W. Va., Aug. 15, 1872.

Children—Lucy Adelaide, b. in Ashtabula, O., May 1, 1832:

Ethelbert Fairchild, b. in Clarksburg, W. Va., July 3 or 5. 1843; Orlando Gorton, b. 1845, d. 1846; Harra Clinton, b. in Clarksburg, W. Va., Nov. 21, 1848; Orlando Wilton, b. in Clarksburg, W. Va., July 18, 1850; Duane S., b. in Clarksburg, W. Va., Aug. 27, 1852, m. Lizzie W. Chamberlain in South Bend, Ind., Apr. 13 or 14, 1879; Inda May, b. 1854, d. 1858; Nellie Scovill, b. Feb. 22, 1857.

32 DUANE BARNES.

Duane Barnes, s. of Elisha Barnes (17), b. at Long Hill, Middletown, Ct., Feb 18, 1814, d. in Middletown, Ct., Sept. 22, 1900, m. Cynthia Sexton Turner. Apr. 20, 1834. She was b. in Middletown, Middlefield, Ct., July 17, 1815, d. Sept. 22, 1867.

Children—Marilla, b. in Long Hill, Ct., June 22, 1835; Llewellyn, b. in Long Hill; Middletown, Ct., Aug. 29, 1836, was wounded and taken prisoner at the battle of Cedar Creek by the Confederates Oct. 19, 1864, and was never afterwards heard from; Hinda, b. in Middletown, Ct., June 13, 1839; Zadell, b. in Middletown, Ct , March 9, 1841; Lillian, b. in Middletown, Ct., Aug. 20, 1844, d. 1845; Reno, b. in Middletown, Ct., Dec. 9, 1845; Gaybert, b. in Middletown, Ct., Oct. 10, 1848; d. in Brooklyn, N. Y., Oct. 13, 1895; Culmer. b. in Middletown, Ct., Aug. 23, 1850; Kilmeny, b. Sept. 17, 1852; Justa, b. 1854, d. 1855; Everet, b. 1859. Duane Barnes m. a second wife, Frances Tibbals.

Children—Urlan, b. in Middletown, Ct., Sept. 19, 1870, d. Jan. 25, 1888; Niar, b. in Middletown, Ct., Feb. 14. 1873; Unade, b. in Middletown, Ct., May 22, 1884.

50 ELIZUR BARNES.

Elizur Barnes, s. of Elizur Barnes (20), b. at Middletown, March 29, 1817, m. Grace Harriet Bevins Oct. 28, 1837. She was b. Nov. 27, 1816, d. Nov. 29, 1886.

Children—Harriet Grace, b. in Hartford, Ct., Feb. 4, 1841, m. Leslie L. Lathrop, in Milwaukee, Wis., Aug.

12, 1873; George Stores Barnes, b. in Hartford, Ct., Oct. 1, 1843, m. Grace Harriet July 2, 1873; Charles Elizur Barnes, b. in Hartford, Ct., July 16, 1847, m. Emma Hardy in Salem, Mass., Apr. 3, 1873; Ellen Amelia, b. in Hartford, Ct., Oct. 30, 1849, d. Nov. 23, 1893, m. Loring L. Tucker Jan. 18, 1893; Ida Isabel, b. in Dorchester, Mass., Jan. 23, 1856, m. Eben E. Robinson May 3, 1876.

66 ETHELBERT F. BARNES.

Ethelbert F. Barnes, s. of Asher Fairchild Barnes (31), b. in Clarksville, W. Va., July 3 or 5, 1843, m. Urana Louderback in Dales, Texas, Oct. 25, 1877. She was b. in Marion, O., July 31, 1859.

Children—Harry Madison, b. in Dallas, Texas, Sept. 8, 1878; Walter Scoville, b. in Dallas, Texas, April 18, 1880; Ethelbert Fairchild, b. in Dallas, Texas, Oct. 22, 1882; Elsie Adeline, b. in Dallas, Texas, July 12, 1885; Burnard Lee, b. in Greer Co., Oklahoma, Aug. 26, 1889; Rosa Lee, b. in Greer Co., Oklahoma, Aug. 26, 1891; Nellie Urana, b. in Greer Co., Oklahoma, Sept. 5, 1894.

68 HARRY CLINTON BARNES.

Harry Clinton Barnes, s. of Asher Fairchild Barnes (31), b. in Clarksburg, W.Va., Nov. 21, 1848, m. Celia H. Neil in Cleveland, O., May 10, 1882.

69 ORLANDO WILTON BARNES.

Orlando Wilton Barnes, s. of Asher Fairchild Barnes (31), b. in Clarksville, W. Va., July 13, 1850, m. Olive L. Dilly in Chicago, Ill., September 6, 1882. She was b. Nunda, McHenry Co., Ill.

Children—Robert Earl, b. in Gurnee, Lake Co., Ill., July 14, 1883; Arthur Clinton, b. in Elgin, Kane Co., Ill., Oct. 8, 1888.

74 MARILLA BARNES CAMERON.

Marilla Barnes, dan. of Duane Barnes (32), b. in Long

Hill, Middletown, Ct., June 22, 1835, m. Derwin De Forest July 7, 1863. He was s. of Curtis DeForest and Emily Barnes. They were divorced in 1865 or 1867. She m. Norman Harriman Bruce in 1870. He died July 12, 1895. She m. Malcolm Cameron in Middletown, Ct., Dec. 1, 1895.

76 HINDA BARNES ROBERTS

Hinda Barnes, dau. of Duane Barnes (32), b. in Middletown, Ct., June 13, 1839, m. George Litch Roberts in Middletown, Ct., Dec. 1, 1865. He was s. of Reuben Roberts and Jane Litch. He was b. in Boston, Mass., Dec. 30, 1836; was graduated A. B. at Wesleyan University June 22, 1859; was admitted to the Suffolk Bar, Boston, Mass., June 7, 1864, councilor of Supreme Court of United States Apr. 1. 1870.

Children—Odin Barnes Roberts, b. in Boston, Mass., June 2, 1867; was graduated A. B. at Harvard University June 30, 1886; was graduated S. B. at Mass. Inst. Technology May 29, 1888; was graduated A. M. and L. L. B. at Harvard University June 24, 1891; admitted to the Suffolk Bar Boston, Mass., Jan. 20, 1891.

Harold Barnes Roberts, b. in Boston, Mass., Aug. 8, 1869, was graduated S. B. at Mass. Inst. of Technology June 3, 1890.

77 ZADEL BARNES GUSTAFSON.

Zadel Barnes, dau. of Duane Barnes (32), b. in Middletown, Ct., March 9, 1841, m. Henry Aaron Buddington Oct. 26, 1857.

Children—Justin Llewellyn, b. in Middletown, Ct., Aug. 22, 1859; Henry, b. in Greenfield, Mass., Jan. 14, 1865.

She was divorced March, 1877; m. Axel Gustafson Middletown, Ct., May 3, 1878. He was b. in Sweden May 3, 1848.

79 REON BARNES.

Reon Barnes, s. of Duane Barnes (32), b. in Middletown, Ct., Dec. 9, 1845; m. Martha Evans Fuller in Norwich, Ct., March 30, 1872. She was the dau. of Ebenezer Fuller; b. in Norwich, Ct., Jan. 13, 1850, d. Dec. 23, 1884.

Children—Reon Barnes, Jr., b. in Staten Island, N. Y., Aug. 3, 1873; Martha Cynthia Barnes, b. in Staten Island, N. Y., Sep. 11, 1875; Alice Twombly Barnes, b. in Staten Island, N. Y., Jan. 9, 1882.

80 GAYBERT BARNES.

Gaybert Barnes, s. of Duane Barnes (32), b. in Middletown, Ct., Oct. 10 1848; d. Oct. 13, 1895. He was of the class of 1869 Wesleyan University, Middletown, Ct.; left college during senior year, received honorary degree of A. M., Wesleyan University in 1876. He m. Mary Louisa Fuller Jan 16, 1872. She was the dau. of Ebenezer Fuller and Harriet Bolles. She was b. in Norwich, Ct., March 22, 1844.

Children—Bessie, b. in New York city March 15, 1873; Rachel, b. in New York city Dec. 21, 1874; Sarah, b. in New York city Feb. 5, 1876; Duane, b. in New York city Oct. 29, 1877, went to Manila. P. I., as private in the 1st Cav. Volunteers May, 1898, died in San Francisco, Cal., Sept. 13, 1899, buried at Middletown, Ct., Sept. 24, 1899; Ebenezer Fuller, b. in New York city Oct. 26, 1879; Annie Mariah, b. in Brooklyn, N. Y., Aug. 24, 1882.

81 CULMER BARNES.

Culmer Barnes, s. of Duane Barnes (32), b. in Middletown, Ct., Aug. 23, 1850, m. Amelia, dau. of Jessie Rodman and Jane Demorest, in Brooklyn, N. Y., May 7, 1874. She was born in Williamsburg, N. Y. June 5, 1854.

Children—Culmer Barnes, Jr., b. in New York city March 11, 1875; Hardin, b. in New York city Aug. 16, 1876; Jessie, b. in New York city Oct. 1, 1878; Elisha, b. in New York city Oct. 24, 1880; Hazel, b. in Sing

Sing, N. Y., Oct. 24, 1890; May Belle, b. in Sing Sing,
N. Y., May 3, 1892.   He died in Sing Sing, N. Y., May
5, 1892; was buried in Middletown, Ct.

82 Kilmeny Barnes Holt.

Kilmeny Barnes, dau. of Duane Barnes (32), b. Sept.
17, 1852, m. Albert Alfonso Holt Sept. 17, 1878.   He was
b. in Amherst, N. Y., July 11, 1845.

84 Everet Barnes.

Everet Barnes, s. of Duane Barnes (32), b. in Middle-
town, Ct., Jan. 24, 1859, m. Sarah Louise Meyers in
New York city March 4, 1893.   She was b. in Saratoga
Springs, N. Y., Nov. 29, 1869.

Children—Margaret Moore Barnes, b. in Brooklyn,
N. Y., Dec. 8, 1893; Mildred Yates Barnes, b. in Sing
Sing, N. Y., Dec. 14, 1895; Everet Barnes, Jr., b in
Sing Sing, N. Y., Dec. 1, 1900.

112 Martha Cynthia Barnes Roberts.

Martha C. Barnes, dau. of Reon Barnes (79), b. Sept.
11, 1875, m. Harold Barnes Roberts in Staten Island,
N. Y., Aug. 14, 1895.   He was s. of Hinda Barnes and
George Litch Roberts, b. in Boston Aug. 8, 1869.

Children—Llewellyn Barnes Roberts, b. in W. Roxbury, Mass., June 10, 1896; Elwin Barnes Roberts, b.
in Hyde Park, Mass., Jan. 10, 1899.

113 Alice Twombly Barnes Lawrence.

Alice Twombly Barnes, dau. of Reon Barnes (79), b.
Jan. 9, 1882, m. Joseph D. Lawrence, Jr., at Staten
Island, N. Y., Aug. 9, 1900.

115 Bessie Barnes Galloway.

Bessie Barnes, dau. of Gaybert Barnes (80), b. in New
York city March 15, 1873, m. Franklin Albert Galloway
in Brooklyn, N. Y., Aug. 18, 1895.   He was born in
Martinsburg, Lewis Co., N. Y., June 4 1867, was graduated A. B. at Wesleyan University June, 1894.

Children—George Barnes Galloway, b. in Brooklyn, N. Y., Jan. 9, 1898; Bessie Galloway, b. in Passaic, N. J., Sept. 17, 1900.

116 Rachel Barnes Little.

Rachel Barnes, dau. of Gaybert Barnes (80), b. in New York city Dec. 21, 1874, m. Charles Eugene Little, Jr., Aug. 18, 1895. He was b. at Nyack, N. Y., April 7, 1873.

Children—Constance Miriam Little, b. in Jersey City, N. J., May 24, 1896; Gaybert Barnes Little, b. in Jersey City, N. J., Aug. 31, 1898.—*Compiled by the author from ".Incestry and Descendants of Shamger Barnes" by George Litch Roberts.*

DESCENDANTS OF TIMOTHY BARNES.

Timothy Barnes, b. in England 16—, d. in Conn.

Timothy Barnes, s. of Timothy, of England, b. in Conn 17 –, d. at Hartford, Conn.

Timothy Barnes, s. of Timothy of Hartford, b. at Hartford, Conn., Apr. 19, 1749, d. at Litchfield, Conn., Oct. 11, 1825, a soldier in the Rev. war, m. Eunice Munson.

Timothy Barnes, s. of Timothy of Litchfield, b. at Litchfield, Conn., Oct. 8, 1780, a soldier of the war of 1812; capt. of militia many years; m. Betsey Cole Sept. 12, 1802, m. Almira Cole, Feb. 3, 1821.

Lemuel Munson Barnes, s. of Timothy, of Conn., b. at Barnes, Pa., Oct. 28, 1831, m. Rachel Call, moved to Sand Beach, Mich.

Lemuel Call Barnes, B. A., s. of Lemuel M. Barnes, b. at Kirtland, O., Nov. 6, 1854; a Baptist minister; resided at Newton Center, Mass —*See American Ancestry.*

CHAPTER IX.
BIOGRAPHICAL SKETCHES.

SUCCESSFUL MEN WHOSE ANCESTRY IS UNKNOWN TO
THE AUTHOR.

RUFUS BARNES.
Successful Pioneer Farmer.

RUFUS BARNES, born near New Haven, Ct., in 1765, married Anna Frisby, moved to Oneida Co., N. Y., and bought a farm near Rome, where he died in 1847. He was one of the pioneers of Oneida County; had two sons, Albert and Ambrose.

AMBROSE BARNES was born near Rome, N. Y., in 1807, where he died in 1851. He had two daughters. Lydia, died when sixteen years old, and Julia who married S. F. Tremain and resides at Rome, N. Y.

ALBERT BARNES.
Theologian and Biblical Commentator.

ALBERT BARNES, oldest son of Rufus Barnes, was born near Rome, N. Y., Dec. 1, 1798; graduated at Hamilton college, at Clinton, N. Y., in 1820, and three years afterwards graduated at the Theological Seminary, Princeton, N. J. He was installed pastor of the Presbyterian Church at Morristown, N. J., Feb. 28, 1825 ; was called to the first Presbyterian Church in Philadelphia in 1830, and was pastor of that church thirty seven years. He is better known as a commentator than as a clergyman. More than a million copies of his commentaries were sold previous to his death, and the demand since then has been as great as it was before. He died in Philadelphia, Pa., Dec. 24, 1870. His children were Albert Henry, James Nathan and Charlotte. They all died in Philadelphia, leaving no children.

HORACE BARNES.
Farmer.

HORACE BARNES, born at Warwick, Mass., about 1800, had three brothers, Cypian, Lyman and Joseph, and four sisters. About 1840 he was married and moved to Bristol, Ill., at which place he died in 1880. He had five children. His sons were Orton A., Harlan P. and A. H.

ORTON A. BARNES.
Jurist and Farmer.

ORTON A. BARNES served three years in the army in the War of the Rebellion; married Eunice Pierce at Paw Paw. Ill.. in about 1867; moved to Memphis, Mo., upon a farm where he died in 1898. He was County Judge several years; had one son, Orton A. Barnes, Jr.. and five daughters.

H. P. BARNES.
Farmer.

H. P. BARNES, son of Horace Barnes, engaged in farming, lives on the old farm at Bristol, Ill.; was married in 1873 to Fannie Bradford of Boston, Mass.; has no children living; has been chairman of the County board of Supervisors many years.

A. H. BARNES.
Proprietor and publisher of The Eagle Grove Eagle.

A. H. BARNES, youngest son of Horace Barnes, was married in 1873 to Lizzie Raymond at Bristol, Ill. They went in 1882 to Miner, S. D.; farmed until 1896 then went to Eagle Grove, Io., and bought the Eagle Grove Eagle which he is now pub-

lishing. They have three sons, as follows:
Horace R., married Ida Humphry at Miner, S. D., in 1895, has two sons, Clarence
and Glenn, is a farmer; Solon A., born in
1867, has an appointment at Washington.
D. C.; Harlan W, born in 1884.

JAMES BARNES.
Soldier and Engineer.

JAMES BARNES, born at Boston, Mass., in 1806; graduated
at West Point in 1829; was appointed brigadier-general in
1862, and brevet major-general U. S. volunteers March 13,
1865. He was wounded at Gettysburg, and died in Springfield, Mass., Feb. 12, 1869, from disease contracted in the
service.

JOSEPH K. BARNES.
Celebrated Soldier and Surgeon.

JOSEPH K. BARNES, born in Philadelphia, Pa., July 21, 1817,
graduated at Harvard College; received his degree of M. D.
from the University of Pennsylvania, class of 1839; was brigadier-general; received the appointment of surgeon-general
Aug. 22, 1864; died at Washington, D. C., 1883.

CHARLES RIED BARNES.
Celebrated Botanist.

CHARLES R. BARNES, M. A. Ph. D., was born in Madison,
Ind., Sep. 7, 1858; educated at Hanover College and Harvard
University; prophessor of botany in the University of Wis
consin. *Johnson's Enc.*

SUPPLEMENT TO CHAPTER V.

CHARLES HENRY WEST. See P. 146.

CHARLES HENRY WEST and SARAH EMILY
BARNES, daughter of Isaac Barnes, were
married at Brighton, Monroe Co., N. Y.,
Dec. 7, 1830; moved to Ridgeway, N. Y.;
had five children, as follows: Daniel Miller, Isaac Barnes, Elisha Yale, Charles
Henry and Elisha Yale, 2nd.

DANIEL MILLER WEST, born Oct. 27, 1831,
died at Prescott, Wis., Apr. 15, 1859.

ISAAC BARNES WEST, born at Ridgeway.
N. Y., June 21, 1833, married Mary Emma
Case at Kingsboro, N. Y., Oct. 3, 1861,
died Apr. 31, 1869. Their children were
Daniel Miller, died in infancy, and Charles
Case.

CHARLES CASE WEST, born Feb. 25, 1867,
resides at 39 First St., Rochester, N. Y., is a
dealer in coal and wood. He married Grace
D. Tibbetts at Gloversville, N. Y., Oct. 19,
1892. They have had three children as follows: Paul J. born Sep. 8, 1895; Margaret

Estella ,born March 1, 1899, died July 14, 1900 ; Ruth Elizabeth, born Sep. 26, 1901.

ELISHA YALE WEST, born Nov. 28, 1835, died March 28, 1849.

CHARLES HENRY WEST, born at Kingsboro, N. Y., Feb. 4, 1839, enlisted in July, 1862, received a lieutenant's commission, was lost at the battle of Ream's Station, Va., Aug. 25, 1864.

ELISHA YALE WEST was born June 2, 1850, at Ridgeway, N. Y., where he now resides.

SUPPLEMENT TO CHAPTER VI.

DESCENDANTS OF JEDEDIAH BARNES.

PHILO EATON, dau. of Jedediah Barnes (see P. 165), had five children, as follows : Mrs. Roxana Hines, Ilion, N. Y. ; Mariah ; Annette ; Allen, employed in the Treasury Dept., Washington, D. C. ; Volney of Herkimer Co., N. Y.

Levi Barnes' Descendants.

CHARLES G. BARNES (see P. 168) m. 2nd

Residence of Levi Barnes. *See P. 166.*

w., Jane Capron, had a son, Levi.

JOHN V. BARNES (see P. 168) m. 1st w., Elizabeth Wellman, 2nd w., Sarah Cupples and 3d w., Jane Messenger; had five children, as follows:

ELLEN A., b. Aug. 4, 1850, m. Mr. Middleton, had three c. Carrie Davidson, Berdinie and Robert.

FRANCIS L., b. Nov. 29, 1853, m. Addie Baybrook, had two c., Nellie B. and Freddie.

ELIZABETH M., b. Sep., 1859, m. William Sears, had three c., Edward b. July 1, 1875, m. Grace Levett, has one c., Hazel; Ella, b. June 23, 1878, m. Lee Davis, has one c., Cecil; Valma, m. Wm. Wellman, has one c., Homer.

ELMER E., b. Nov. 1, 1861, is m. has two or three children.

MARY, b. March 18, 1869, m. Oliver Bryner, has two c., lives at Union City, Pa.

ALPHEUS S. BARNES (see P. 168) had three c., as follows:

FREMONT S., b. Aug. 14, 1857, m. Mary Goodrich, P. O., Scranton, Pa.

J. ARVILLA, b. Jan. 1859, m. Wm. Egbert,

P. O., Union City, Pa.

HARRY ALPHEUS, b. March 28, 1886, P. O., Union City, Pa.

LEVI GALUSHA BARNES (see P. 168) had six children, as follows:

OLIVE A. b. Dec. 19, 1858, m. J. M. Carroll, has two c., Clarence C., b. 1884, and Winnifred, b. 1894.

ALICE M., b. Oct. 3, 1860, m. Fletcher S. Carroll, had three c., Wayne T., b. 1881; Alta M., b. 1889; Mabel L., b. 1893.

MELVA ANN d. young.

MARY R., b. Sep. 17, 1865, m. John W. Donaldson, has one c., Lewis J., b. Dec. 1, 1902.

EMMA, b. Aug. 5, 1867, m. Oscar Clark, has two c., Ross, b. 1889, and Raymond, b. 1891.

JENNIE LYNN, b. March 4, 1872.

SUSAN A. BARNES (see P. 170), b. Apr. 15, 1838, m. George W. Carroll who was born Jan. 29, 1831. They live three miles west of Union City, Pa.; are engaged quite extensively in farming and dairy business.

NATHAN SYLVESTER BARNES—see P. 169.

HANNAH E. MOORE, dau. of Levi Barnes, b. March 6, 1830, d. Apr. 11, 1903, had two children, as follows ·

LILLIE SATERLY, b. Dec. 18, 1870, has four c., Laurence, Mabel, Allene, Bessie.

CORNELIA born Dec. 3, 1872, m. H. H. Chaffee. Their P. O. is Union City, Pa.

SOPHIA, dau. of Levi Barnes, m. Norman Nichols, died May 9, 1893. Mr. Nichols was a soldier in the War of the Rebellion ; died March 2, 1881. They had seven children, as follows:

ELMINA, m. Edgar Earl, c. were Edith, Leonard, Bertha and Roy.

EFFIE, m. Delos Clemons, c. Arthur and Bertha.

LYDIA died young.

SYLVIA, b. March 23, 1855, m. Darwin Hinebaugh, lives at Jamestown, N. Y., c. are Lillie Vandenburg, North Clymer, N. Y. ; George, m. Lizzie Tripp, P. O., Conneaut Lake, Pa. ; Nellie, m. Burt Field, P. O., Fresno, Cal. ; Levi, m. Frances Wells, P. O. Jamestown, N. Y. ; Grace ; Mina, m. Clarence Warner, P. O., Union City, Pa.

ARTHUR, m. Lizzie McCuller, c. Delos. Guy, Eddie, Clem, Nellie, Julius, Baby.

FLORA, m. James Clark, lives in Newton. Illinois.

GERTIE m. Owen Barnes. See P. 169.

SUPPLEMENT TO CHAPTER VII.

HENRY AND LYDIA BROWN. See P. 178.

HENRY BROWN was born near Albion, Pa.. Apr. 1, 1840.

LYDIA BARNES was born in Conneaut Tp., Erie Co., Pa., May 22, 1840.

Henry Brown and Lydia Barnes were married Dec. 27, 1864. Their children are Nora L. ,Katie M., Fred L. and Bonnie B.

NORA L. BROWN was born July 15, 1897.

KATE M. BROWN, b. June 3, 1869, *married* Mark Hills of Crawford Co., Pa.. Nov. 22, 1898, has one daughter, Thelma, born Nov. 21, 1902.

FRED L. BROWN, b. Nov .4, 1871, m. May C. Bigelow of Conneaut, O.. Dec. 27, 1899.

BONNIE B. BROWN, born June 17, 1873, m. Wm. Laughery June 10, 1902.

INDEX.

RR 3.5

LIBRARY OF CONGRESS

ST. AUGUSTINE
FLA.

LIBRARY OF CONGRESS

0 007 394 488 0